read my hips

the *sexy* art
of *flirtation*

EVE MARX

PoLKA DoT
press

Published by

Polka Dot Press, an imprint of Adams Media,
an F+W Publications, Inc. Company
57 Littlefield Street, Avon, MA 02322 USA
www.adamsmedia.com

ISBN: 1-59337-456-9

Printed in the United States of America.
J I H G F E D C B A

Library of Congress Cataloging-in-Publication Data
Marx, Eve.
Read my hips / Eve Marx.
p.   cm.
ISBN 1-59337-456-9
1. Flirting. 2. Man-woman relationships. 3. Women--Conduct of life. I. Title.

HQ801.M2353 2005
646.7'7--dc22

2005005221

This publication is designed to provide accurate and authoritative information with regard to the subject matter covered. It is sold with the understanding that the publisher is not engaged in rendering legal, accounting, or other professional advice. If legal advice or other expert assistance is required, the services of a competent professional person should be sought.

—From a *Declaration of Principles* jointly adopted by a Committee of the American Bar Association and a Committee of Publishers and Associations

Many of the designations used by manufacturers and sellers to distinguish their products are claimed as trademarks. Where those designations appear in this book and Adams Media was aware of a trademark claim, the designations have been printed with initial capital letters.

This book is available at quantity discounts for bulk purchases.

For information, please call 1-800-872-5627.

FOR VAL

ACKNOWLEDGMENTS

In making the book *Read My Hips* possible, I would first like to thank my agent, the always flirtatious June Clark, who put me up for this project with Danielle Chiotti of Polka Dot Press, who willingly embraced it. I also wish to thank all the copyeditors, designers, production, and sales personnel at Adams Media for their professionalism, expertise, and experience.

For answering my e-mails and corresponding so flirtatiously with me, I would like to thank Eileen Murray, Helen Peeples, Roxanne James, Shane Miller, JoAnn Hornak, Vicky Oliver, Susan Reynolds, Linda Stout, Kevin Wright, Suzanne Dennie, Erin Hoffman, Bob O'Malley, and the Blueyedtxcwby with a couple of provocative numbers at the end of his screen name who freely flirted with a total stranger, *moi,* for forty minutes late one night in an AOL chatroom. Thank you, Tony. You really were a dream!

I'd also like to thank my husband, Rick Marx, who puts up with my incorrigible flirting, and my son, Sam, who was the most flirtatious baby I've ever seen. I still remember the way he climbed right up on women's laps and batted his eyes at them when he was about five years old. Sam, you were a superflirt! I'd also like to thank the German Warmblood horse, Valentine, for persistently teaching me a thing or two about equine-human relations, and the Turkish Van cat, Leo, who is an incredible flirt and boyfriend. Leo, you're the only guy who is so excited by me that you actually drool. Thank you.

On a very personal note, I would like to thank the members of the very unofficial Perks Morning Flirt Club, Joshua Katz, Tom Dawson, Kit Combes, Leslie Scott, Richard C., Ed Giobbi, Rani, Bahman Soltani, Andrzej Krakowski, Marc Black, Barbara Gatfield, Barbara Misiano, Marc Jaffe, Lorna Whittemore, Elena, Larry Wolhandler (when he can make it), and the real cowboy, Chris DeFilippis, who cofounded the flirt team with me. Each and every one of you enlivens my mornings. I don't know how I would make it through the day without you. *Mwah!*

INTRODUCTION

A truly *accomplished* flirt
can flirt with anything . . .
as long as it's breathing.

Birds do it, bees do it, babies do it, horses, cats, old people, young people, married, single, tall, short, fat, and skinny people do it. . . . What is it that they all do? Flirt! My trusty *Merriam-Webster's Dictionary* says flirt is a verb meaning "to behave amorously without serious intent" or "to show casual interest.""

My whole life, people have joked that if you look up the word *flirt* in any dictionary, you will find my name. Even though my name isn't actually listed among the definitions of the word, I am undoubtedly a flirt. I was probably flirting right from the cradle. For as long as I can remember, I've flirted with dogs, horses, cats, canaries, and a whole slew of human beings, most of whom have flirted right back! Flirting is in my blood. You could say the behavior is hardwired into my DNA.

Although some people (mostly curmudgeonly cranks) do consider my nonstop habit of flirting to be irregular, if not downright unseemly, I would venture to say that who I am and what I have achieved is all due to flirting. You could say I am a bona fide Flirtation Expert. That is why I decided to write this book—so I could pass on my years of experience to you, dear readers.

So much of good flirting is simply being charming. My ability to flirt and to charm has helped me, even guided me, every step of my way.

I make it my business to flirt every day. As a writer who specializes in the subjects of human behavior (and sex!) I consider flirting to be an essential part of my workday. Flirting is the thing that jump-starts me and helps me get jazzed to do all the tough work (and, *groan,* the tedious chores) that make up my regular day. Hopefully after you read this book, you'll feel that way, too!

Flirting is really good medicine, at least as good as chicken soup—to that I can attest. Recently when I was down with the flu and freaking out over all the tasks on my to-do list, I dragged myself out of bed for a large cup of green tea. I found the only thing that perked me up and galvanized me was flirting. Just like those zinc tablets I was popping like Pez candies to push through the flu, some quick jolts of flirting made me feel more like myself again. I remember that particular morning at the coffee bar where I do my daily flirting and watch other people flirt, the dark, silent beauty sitting on the bench to the left of me relayed to all of us sitting there that a man who could make her laugh was the one who would get her, which touched off a furious round of hilarious flirting.

I truly believe flirting is an art, and through this book, I hope to pass on some of that art to you. Certainly the great geishas and courtesans and concubines of past centuries and cultures understood this. They applied their art not only for their own financial security and to maintain their social positions, but also because they grasped the significant role of flirting in society at large. Under the guise of flirting, important information got passed from one person to another when honor, politics, and entire fortunes were at stake. As a consequence of flirting, undoubtedly in some circles necks were saved or heads were lost on the guillotine! In Japanese culture, if a husband had an affair, it was hurtful. But if a husband was involved with a geisha, it was an honor. An HONOR. The main rule you need to remember as you read this book, and in real life, is "Work with what you've got." That means if you're tall, you can be flirtatiously intimidating. If you're petite, play the baby-doll card. If you've got long legs, dress and comport yourself to call attention to them. If you've got a beautiful face, use your eyes and mouth a lot. If you've got an outstanding bosom, keep your shoulders back, stand up straight, and wear clothing that complements or even draws an arrow to your assets.

Though the "art" of flirting may be somewhat lost on modern culture, you can also look at it as a sport or game. As in any sport, how badly you want to win determines how well you'll play. Whether your interest in flirting is to meet a mate, get ahead in your career, improve your social situation, or just refine your skills, you'll be a better flirt after you read this book. Have fun with it. The point of flirting is simple—it's to enjoy life more!

PART ONE

getting *started*

CHAPTER 1

YOU SAY I'M A FLIRT LIKE IT'S A BAD THING

Life's too short not to flirt— at least *a little*

WHAT IS FLIRTING, ANYWAY?

Is it simply being friendly? Will great flirting win you popularity and dates? Can flirting improve your economic status, gain you friends, help you influence people, make you a better person? Can flirting enhance your complexion, help you lose weight, find you a lover, put you in the driver's seat?

The answer to all these questions is an absolute yes! Amazing as it seems, flirting is the one little magic pill that can make a huge difference in your life, if you know how to use it.

PRIMAL FLIRTATIONS

Flirting may actually be hard-wired into all mammals, including the very fuzzy and furry ones. Ever watch two squirrels chase each other up and down a tree? Or how your cats—even if both of them are males—behave around each other? (All that rubbing up against things . . . that's a major cat flirt.)

Babies are natural born flirters as well. Think about it: Babies flirt out of an inborn sense of survival. All those goo-goo eyes and shy looks that say "love me" and "spare me because I'm so adorable" are the beginning of a lifetime of flirtation as a means to an end. By flirting, babies can fulfill their need to be fed and to be loved and nurtured—all integral to survival.

MODERN-DAY FLIRTING

A very flirtatious man once said to me, "Flirting is sex lite." That's a fair analysis. Flirting is a lot like drinking diet soda. It's sexy but it isn't sex. Flirting is like sex without the calories!

The beautiful thing about flirting is that it's like a crime of opportunity. It's all about taking advantage of what is right in front of you. The tools are always there—it's what you do with them that counts. So, as you embark on your fabulous flirting journey, keep in mind that a good flirt prospect is not always the one that is the most obvious. The hottest guy in the room at a party may turn out to be a terrible flirt. Chances are he's so used to women coming on to him that he's lazy and likes to let the woman do all the work. A far better flirt prospect is the guy standing alone who would just love to have someone to talk to. He's the guy you should use your "So, what brings you to this gathering?" line on.

The ABCs of Flirting

Being a great flirt is a little like being a great salesperson. It's a way of getting what you want or even just making the most out of a lousy situation.

The ABCs of flirting are:

Approach

Behavior

Control

A. First, select your flirt quarry and approach him. Your approach can take on many forms. You can try the direct approach—like waving or just walking up and saying hi—or go for an indirect one, like drawing attention to yourself by standing close by yet studiously ignoring that person until it's obvious that you're ignoring him. That means he has to approach *you*.

B. Your behavior can make or break the flirt. Pick a demeanor to work with even if you don't stick with it. Depending on the situation, you could go for friendly, inquisitive, and teasing or mysterious and aloof.

   BIG HINT: Read the other person's body language and mirror it. Monkey see, monkey do. It's amazing how quickly people respond to behavior that mimics their own. And it's so simple to be a copycat. Tee-hee, it's practically child's play!

C. Control is where it's at. The Object of Your Flirtation is to control the situation, even if your control is wielded by making the other person believe that he is the one in charge. How will you know when you've got the upper hand? When the other person is eating out of yours.

So you see, the secret to flirting isn't about great lines (although great lines do help). It isn't about how many phone numbers you collect, or how many notches you cut on your bedpost. The reason to flirt is that flirting enables you to develop a personality that inspires others to want to interact with you. Flirting, like having good posture, is something you become much better at if you commit to working on it all the time. Your flirting can be very subtle. All that's required is that you be charming to other people, regardless of their gender or any special interest you have in them.

Compliment people you think deserve (or could use) a compliment. Be warm and friendly even when there's nothing "in it" for you. Be comfortable with yourself and with others, and the rest will just fall into place. When you stop worrying about whether or not you're any good at flirting, eventually it will become as natural to you as breathing—and as necessary as air to your life force.

FLIRTING IS FOR EVERYONE!

I read somewhere a long time ago that flirting is "attraction without intention." But this isn't entirely true. There must be some intent, even if your intention is just to make yourself feel better. Flirting is one of the few great things you can do to benefit yourself that has the effect of making somebody else feel good, too. When you flirt with someone, even momentarily, you feel better, they feel better, and it's a total win-win situation.

And while we're at it, let's dispel the old myth that flirting is only for single women "on the prowl." Not true! As you've already seen, flirting isn't just about snagging a guy—it's about enhancing your life in all areas. And if you happen to nab a great man in the process, then more power to you!

Married, Not Dead

No matter what you've been told before, you can make flirting part of your "happily ever after." Married people can flirt, should flirt, and in fact, they should especially flirt with each other. Flirting keeps a relationship fresh and spontaneous. Flirting can keep love alive. You know a marriage is on the rocks when the two parties have lost any desire to flirt with each other.

That said, what about flirting with other people when you're married? As long as it's harmless, well, it's harmless. For one thing, life's too short not to flirt. Just because you're married and you're flirting doesn't mean you're actively searching for extracurricular activities. For many normal, well-adjusted people, flirting is the equivalent to drinking a great cup of coffee or sucking on a Hershey's Kiss. It gets you revved up and ready to face the long day.

Casual flirting (i.e., "flirting lite") is a way to exercise your mind, help you feel attractive, and in some cases make you even more attractive to your authorized and legal partner. The trick here is to never be serious.

To be a great flirt, you have to be in great health. And how are you going to be a great flirt without bright, shining eyes? Here are a couple of foods packed with good stuff to keep your eyes a-twinkle:

- Carrots, which contain vitamins A and E, are famous for being good for the eyes.

- Marigold flower extract, also known as lutein, is known to be excellent for the eyes and is said to improve and preserve vision.

- Spinach, rosemary, and blueberries are also known to be excellent for sparkly eyes and improved vision.

Here's a quick list of Dos and Don'ts to get you out there flirting without crossing any marriage or relationship-sensitive lines:

→ DO mention that you are married (or otherwise seriously involved) at some point in the exchange, preferably within the first sixteen sentences. The point of the flirt is for both participants to have fun, not get anybody's hopes up.

→ DON'T make any overtly physical gestures. Aside from briefly touching someone's hand, try to keep it to verbal flirting.

→ DO compliment the other person. Tell him if you like his sweater, his shoes, or his hair. The objective is to spread good feelings around.

→ DON'T engage in hostile, negative verbal sparring. Although it's true that challenging, confrontational flirting does work for some people as a kind of psychological foreplay, if you're not really available and you're just playing someone, your words will come off more as a putdown.

→ DO participate in three-party flirting or flirting in groups. Three-party flirting is where you flirt with more than one person at a time, but you also use another person to help you with your flirt. You use his or her energy to augment your own and double your power! This is an excellent opportunity to enhance your own flirting skills while helping someone else hook up.

→ DON'T drink and flirt. If you're married and your spouse is out of town, this could definitely lead to trouble.

→ DO lay your cards on the table that you're not actually available if the other person brings it up right away.

→ DON'T try to bluff and obscure the fact that you're married if you are.

→ DO flirt with as many people as possible if you're at a party or public place. If you flirt obviously with everyone, including babies, old people, other women, and dogs, no one can accuse you of attempting to hijack her spouse.

→ DON'T flirt with your neighbor's husband if you don't get along with your neighbor.

→ DO flirt with other happily married people if you are happily married yourself. Actually, this makes for some of the best flirting. Somehow it just frees everyone up when everyone is on the same page.

→ DON'T leave a party with a person you were flirting with, unless it is your spouse. Tongues will wag, and who needs the notoriety?

YOUR FLIRTING STYLE

So, as you incorporate flirting into your life, you should make it a goal to master at least three different flirting styles and have them ready to roll in your flirt vocabulary.

Develop your flirting styles as though they are muscles that need regular exercise to maintain tone. In other words, flex, flex, flex! There are so many ways to flirt, and if you're having trouble figuring out your flirting style or you just need some inspiration, try these on for size:

IS HE FLIRT WORTHY?

Even if you are an insatiable flirt who will flirt with just about anything in pants, it's definitely a waste of your talent and your energy to flirt with someone who is just not worth the effort! Before you straighten your shoulders, suck in your tummy, and toss back your hair, size up your flirt quarry and determine if he's worth it.

Here are the important questions:

Q: *Do you think he is appealing/attractive/someone you'd like to get to know?*
A: If you don't find him suitably attractive, the only good reason to flirt him up is to practice your skills. Just think of what you're doing in a theatrical way—sort of like "running lines."

Q: *When you cast an arched-eyebrow look his way, does he steadily* return your gaze?
A: When you telegraph him your best "are you interested look," if he gives you a similar look back, you're in like Flint.

Q: *If he was the first one looking, how interested did he appear?*
A: He looked first? Good. Just keep repeating to yourself, "He pursued me."

Q: *What is his body language telling you about him? Does he look open and interested?*
A: Don't even bother flirting with a guy with bad posture. If he can't be bothered to stand up straight, how's he going to pay attention to you?

Q: Once you've engaged him in some conversation, is he holding up his end?

A: Flirting is a lot like a game of tennis. The longer you can keep the conversational volley going, the better the flirting is. If he misses all your lobs or keeps rushing the net, whack the ball at him and just walk away!

Q: If his arms are crossed in front of his chest, is it because he's a bit shy and defensive or is he sending you a warning to stay away?

A: The arms over the chest thing is nearly impossible to read. You'll have to focus on his eyes instead. If he's making lots of eye contact, he's telling you to keep talking, persevere, and proceed. If he's glancing around the room or staring at the floor, he's probably sending the No Trespass message—so get off the property and move on to something (or someone) else!

Q: Are his eyes on you, and only you, or does his gaze wander from skirt to skirt?

A: A guy who is looking at you like you're the only woman in the room is a guy worth flirting with. A guy whose eyes follow every woman in the room is just a dog whose name is Rover.

Q: Is he wearing a wedding band?

A: You can flirt with a married man—a little. In fact, they often make the best flirts. Just keep your flirting light and enjoy the repartee. If he asks for your phone number, you better point out his ring status!

Q: If you're flirting with him online, how fast does he respond to your IMs (instant messages)?

A: Some guys take a really long time responding to IM. That could mean you're flirting with someone whose wife or girlfriend is in the bathroom. If he signs off abruptly, you know he's just been caught!

Q: How fast does he type?

A: You know that old saying, small hands, small you-know-what? Well, a guy who is a fast typist is usually a very worthy flirt.

→ *The Blond Flirt* (think Marilyn Monroe)

→ *The Girl Next Door Flirt* (think Mary Ann from *Gilligan's Island*)

→ *The Dark Beauty* (think Julia Roberts in *Closer*)

→ *Dominatrix Lite* (think Demi Moore in *Disclosure*)

→ *Married Flirt* (think Brittany Murphy in *Just Married*)

→ *Shy Flirt* (think Natalie Portman in *Star Wars*)

→ *The Wide-Eyed Beauty* (think Scarlett Johansson in *Lost in Translation*)

→ *Reticent Flirt* (think Virginia Madsen in *Sideways*)

→ *Outrageous Flirt* (think Debra Messing, in anything!)

→ *Sexy Flirt* (think Cameron Diaz in *Being John Malkovich*)

→ *Mature Cool Flirt* (think Diane Lane in *Unfaithful*)

→ *Tough Flirt* (think Sigourney Weaver, period)

→ *Seductive Flirt* (think Helena Bonham Carter in *Howards End*)

Speaking of actresses, to be a great flirt it doesn't hurt if you can occasionally be one. Every woman has it within her power to be an actress. Even if you failed to land a part in a high school play and standup comedy isn't your shtick, you can channel the gestures and the dialogue of some of the great performers in classic, and even less than classic, films. Think of Katharine Hepburn, who flirted with her real-life boyfriend Spencer Tracy in *Desk Set,* mostly by going against type and playing the antiflirt! Or Julie Christie flirting with Warren Beatty in *Shampoo.* Still doubtful?

Think of Meg Ryan in just about any role. . . . Think how she flirted up Kevin Kline in *French Kiss,* or Tom Hanks in *Sleepless in Seattle,* or that big flirtatious fake orgasm thing she did to a captivated and yet horrified Billy Crystal in *When Harry Met Sally.* Marvelous Meg flirts magnificently even when her face is all swollen up from crying and she's wearing a dowdy bathrobe.

If movie actresses leave you cold, try channeling some great real-life flirts you have admired. Think about the great flirts you've observed and admired in your own life. Your mother? Your sister? That girl who sat across from you in algebra who all the boys adored? Channel their energy and recall exactly what they said and did that made them such great flirts. Feel free to borrow from their repertoire of techniques. There's no need to "reinvent the wheel." When in doubt, just steal!

Finally, let me leave you with this one piece of advice that has worked for me time and time again: FLIRT MORE—BE HAPPY! Trust me, it works like a charm.

CHAPTER 2

LOCATION! LOCATION!

"As long as you *dare*, it don't matter *where*."

In flirting and in real estate, the rules are the same: Location is everything! Once you get in the habit of looking at nearly every physical location and situation as an opportunity to flirt, you'll quickly realize the only thing you need is a warm body. How can a girl possibly be flirtatious, you ask, when she's been standing in line for an hour at the Department of Motor Vehicles, or watching her clothes go round and round at the Laundromat? It's sooooooo much easier to get a good flirtation going in a dull and even dingy place instead of someplace more predictable, like a bar or nightclub. Why? Because flirting is so unexpected in a dirty old Laundromat that you are 100 percent certain to catch your cute quarry off guard!

A Little Flirtation Goes a Long Way

Think you don't have enough opportunities to flirt? Think again. Taking advantage of location is one of the best flirtation tactics you can employ. By working with the situation at hand, like Lindsay did, you'll find opportunities in even the most mundane places:

Lindsay was living in a miniscule apartment in Greenwich Village and loving her single life. The only thing missing (besides a boyfriend) was a washer and dryer. Sick of rinsing her underwear in the bathroom sink, she hauled her clothing over to the little neighborhood coin-op joint across the street week after week, hating every minute of it.

One day, while she was monitoring her spin cycle, a super hot guy came in and smiled at her as he loaded a washing machine. As Lindsay looked around the room, she noticed there was no shortage of hot women and men doing their laundry. It was a veritable smorgasbord of flirtation opportunities!

Since hardly anyone in the neighborhood had their own appliances, sooner or later nearly everyone within a four-block radius showed their face at the laundry. On any given evening or weekend Lindsay could count on running into at least one of her friends and any number of hot guys. It was a like a singles bar, only without liquor.

Even if you are just going to the *Laundromat*, always wear lipstick. It increases your *flirt-a-liciousness*!

One dull Tuesday evening when she was doing her laundry, a super-hottie wearing a cowboy hat walked through the door, carrying a major load of laundry. Lindsay discreetly eyeballed him as he piled his duds in the washer, paying attention to the important stuff, like that all his things were guy things—no women's clothing or lingerie, and no little kid stuff. In short, he was perfect flirting material. At the very least she figured flirting him up would make the time pass faster.

From behind her magazine, she checked out his butt. His body language told her he was not completely unaware of her existence. True, he kept his back turned, but his movements were a bit self-conscious, like he knew he was being watched.

Always be prepared.
Carry change.   Carry matches.
A pair of jumper cables can come in handy, too.
Who says *you can't flirt*
while doing a *good deed*?

Lindsay was just wondering how to break the ice when the perfect flirtation opportunity presented itself. She knew she had him when she saw him fish for change in his pockets, only to realize that all he had was dollar bills.

"Need change?" she said sweetly, coming to the rescue.

As soon as he got his washer going, he asked if she had time for a drink. "Um, maybe," she said, casting a reluctant eye in the direction of her laundry, which was still going round and round. He quickly took charge of the situation and loped across the street to the liquor store, returning after a few minutes with a bottle of champagne, complete with plastic glasses!

They sipped champagne as they dried their clothes, and had a pleasant conversation. At the end of the night when the sexy cowboy asked for her number, Lindsay was glad to give it.

By making the most of her location, Lindsay lucked into a fabulous situation. There are endless possibilities out there, and as a true flirt, it's your mission to find them.

WORKING YOUR LOCATION

Being an expert flirt means thinking on your feet. Styling your flirt technique to a specific location is key to success. You must be able to adjust your flirting based on the situation at hand. For example, your body language when you're sitting at a bar is radically different from your body language when you're taking a hike in the woods. This entire section is devoted to giving you pointers for every situation, so you'll always be on your toes.

At the Bar

Ah, the classic flirtation situation. When you're flirting in a bar, you've got to exude confidence. Don't be afraid to use your body. Cross and uncross your legs. Toss your hair. Play with your swizzle stick, or catch a guy's stare and hold it. Lick your lips. Bite your lips. Massage your own upper arms. The one thing you don't want to do is twiddle your thumbs, unless you're trying to send some dude a message that you wish he'd get lost!

The Great Outdoors

What's more romantic than a walk in the woods? Okay, this may be a little too Grizzly Adams for you, but if you're into nature, going for a hike is an excellent flirting opportunity. Hold out your hand for balance and assistance—this is a safe gesture but it also gets you pressing flesh against flesh. Shiver! Act like you're cold so he'll give you his coat—or better yet, hug you. Nothing like good old body heat to warm things up.

Traffic Jams

Just because you're stuck in traffic doesn't mean you can't make the most of it. Don't worry—you don't need to drive a snazzy sports car to flirt in traffic jams. Seize the opportunity to hone your flirting skills by checking out the people in the lane next to you. If you spot a cutie, smile helplessly and tilt your head in a "What can you do?" manner. What's the worst than can happen? Chances are he will smile right back!

Traffic jams are also a wonderful opportunity to perfect your Flirtation Gaze (please see glossary for full definition). Make eye contact with the guy in the car behind you by studying your rearview mirror. Get his attention, but don't hold his gaze for too long. If you're feeling extra flirty, flash a smile or give a little wave. But remember, what you want to do is have fun, not have him follow you off the freeway. If this happens, pretend you have no idea why he followed you, and keep your hand on your cell phone!

The Coffee Shop

Coffee bars are great places to flirt, especially if the tables are set close together and there are plenty of magazines and newspapers strewn about. There's no better place to strike up a conversation with a handsome stranger than while sipping your iced Americano at your local coffee joint.

When are you *flirting* and when are you just being *friendly*?
The first step to both is to reach out to someone and instigate a connection.
Where you take it from there is up to you!

Offer to share your newspaper or to move over to make space. Smile at the cute guy waiting his turn for the half-and-half. Say "Good morning" as you stir in your sugar. Or play it totally the opposite way and be mysterious. Write in your journal. Focus on your laptop. Let someone else make the first move and then wow them with your million-dollar charm.

Is That Book Any Good?

Bookstores (and bookstore cafés) are amazing places to flirt. If you're looking for a motorcycle bad boy, stroll on over to the automobile section. If you're a pet lover, hang out in the pet book section to meet guys who are into their pets. Another interesting place to strike up conversation is in the travel section. Who knows, you might meet the guy who will take you on your next great trip! Also, don't overlook the possibilities of the reference section or where they keep all the books that tell you how to study for some tough test. You might meet an incredible lawyer in the making looking at the LSAT practice tests or a future doctor studying for the MCAT. Avoid talking to guys in the section for poets and writers unless you have a weakness for men who expect you to go Dutch. Writers never make any money, and poets—they make even less!

The Grocery Store

Where they keep the meat is where it's at when it comes to flirting in the grocery store. Men, remember, are principally carnivores! The most obvious thing to say to a man you've eyeballed in the meat department is to ask for cooking tips. Favored flirt jump-starts are, "Can you tell me the difference between sirloin and shell steak?" Or, "Which of these cuts do you think is the most tender?" If you play your cards right, the guy may even offer to do the cooking for you. What could be better? P.S. If you hate red meat, do this same shtick in the fish or poultry section.

EXTRACTING PERSONAL INFORMATION FROM A FLIRTATION SESSION (FLIRTING WITH PURPOSE)

Flirting just for the sake of flirting or to pass the time of day is entirely different from flirting with a purpose. If your purpose is not simply to reassure yourself that you're:

A. adorable, and
B. very clever

but to glean Important Personal Information from your flirt subject, there are ways to pose your questions or comments in such a manner that you could get a job as a private investigator! Policemen very often use this tactic by asking very few direct questions and concentrating on small talk.

Small talk, by the way, is the backbone of flirtatious dialogue. If you can amiably chat about the weather, yak about your pet, make cute jokes about your various relatives, well, you're halfway to being a first-class flirt—and that's without even trying.

So there!

Working the *Damsel in Distress* angle can work to your benefit with some men, but use this tactic *sparingly*— you don't want to give the impression that you're too high maintenance.

FLIRTATIOUS PICK-UP LINES
SUITABLE FOR VARIOUS LOCATIONS

Opportunities to have an exchange with other people sometimes happen in the most ordinary spots. A flirtation artiste should be able to pick up on small cues or signals to adapt her stance and her manner to almost any situation. The following lines are specially formulated for flirtations of varying conditions and circumstance:

IN THE BOUTIQUE FOOD MARKET: "Which cheese do you think goes better with pinot grigio?"

IN THE PET FOOD STORE: "My dog loves rawhide strips but the vet says they're no good for her. What do you think?"

WHILE WAITING ON THE METRO PLATFORM FOR THE NEXT TRAIN TO COME IN: "Are the trains running late? Do you know what time it is?"

IN A SPORTING-GOODS STORE: "I just started playing golf. Could you recommend a good brand of shoes?"

IN THE AIRPORT WAITING TO BOARD A PLANE: "I love these redeye flights, don't you?" Or, "Could you help me put this in the overhead?"

AT THE GYM OR HEALTH CLUB: "Have you been waiting long for that bench press?"

A key thing you might want to know if you are Flirting with Purpose is the availability status of your flirtee. It's one thing to charmingly banter with an attractive member of the opposite sex for no other reason than he happens to be standing there. It is another thing entirely to flirt in order to ascertain whether or not he's someone you might consider going on a date with.

Here are some phrases you might use to excellent effect to discover whether or not a guy is Available, Married, or Living with Someone:

> "What a cute dog! Does it belong to you?"

> "I love your leather jacket. Did you pick it out by yourself?"

> "My little brother is coming in from blah blah blah to spend the holidays with me. Do you have any fun plans?"

Be very attentive to pronouns when determining your flirtee's availability status. "We" usually indicates that the person is not

Looking for a luxurious way to boost his libido? Caviar contains large amounts of vitamins A, D, B_1, B_2, and B_6 as well as phosphorous, all known stimulants to the system.

single. But men can be very tricky, especially if an appealing woman is flirting with them. They go out of their way to say "I" when they should be saying "we." What you have to do here is pepper them with a lot of questions that have to be answered with a pronoun. If they are trying to be slick, sooner or later they *will* slip up, unless they are very cool characters (and accomplished flirt experts as well).

At the Gym

A flirt-wise woman will heed this advice: Leave your headphones at home! How are you supposed to tune into your surroundings or start a conversation if you're busy playing with your iPod?

Gyms and health clubs are perfect places to start a flirtation. For one thing, you're already half undressed. Take advantage of the facilities and the equipment to ask for help and favors. The gym is an ideal place to be a bit of a damsel in distress. "Can you give me a spot?" is a perfectly natural thing to say as you approach the bench press. Or you can ask a cute guy, "Could you tell me what time the next spin class starts?" Or ask that guy with the Just Came Back from Vacation tan, "Could you show me the way to the tanning tables?"

Galas and Special Events

Contrary to what you may believe, it's not true that every guy who attends a black-tie gala or special event is there with a date. For one thing, many hostesses and chairwomen deliberately invite stags, if only for the express purpose of hooking them up with their own single girlfriends! Don't be surprised if there's actual competition for them among flirtatious women. What do you say to an apparently single man at a gala?

"Would you very much mind freshening my drink?" is a terrific icebreaker.

Another staple at society events is the Photo Op, when all those pictures of all the attendees in dressy clothes are taken, which later grace the party poop pages of all the local newspapers. One way to make a very memorable impression on a man you just met is to thrust yourself in the photographer's way and get your picture taken together. That way days or weeks or even months later when the pictures are published, the guy will say, "Oh, yeah, I remember that woman," and guess what?

Thanks to the photo's caption, he'll even learn your name!

Professional Networking Events and Business Meetings

Networking parties are a great place to meet new people. And even if you don't find a single decent prospect to flirt with, at least you'll get some fresh business cards.

You might think that a business meeting is too serious a place to flirt, but it isn't, if you do it right. This is the perfect situation to show off your business savvy. Take on the role of an authoritative flirt by showing the men in the room your business smarts. You can come on like gangbusters as long as you leave one extra button of your blouse open—it never hurts to captivate with your slight cleavage while you drive your point home! A well-fitting suit is your best attire. It can be completely professional even as it hugs your curves. And don't forget to use your pencil as a pointer. Use it to point to the guy you like best in the room! Don't be afraid to show your smarts. Look at the way Cybill Shepherd wrapped Bruce Willis around her little finger in the TV show *Moonlighting,* which was all about flirtation.

Get Me to the Church on Time

A whole new way to look at church or temple! Okay, obviously you're there for reasons other than flirting. But your place of worship

BUSINESS DOS
AND DON'TS

It's a fine line you walk when you mix business and pleasure. But if you know how to work it, a little flirtation can go a long way. Here are some Dos and Don'ts to make flirting work for you in a business situation:

- **DO** lean forward and do a little bit of talking with your hands.

- **DON'T** be afraid to be a bit saucy, even confrontational. In a business situation, taking that kind of position is expected!

- **DO** make strong eye contact. When you avoid eye contact, you're telling the other person that when the pressure is on, you'll cave.

- **DON'T** cross and uncross your legs often in the workplace. What works great in a bar is way too provocative in the workplace. In this situation, too much leg action indicates you're nervous or, worse, that you need to visit the restroom.

- **DO** mirror the other person's facial expressions. This is a good opportunity to play a little game of Monkey See,

Monkey Do. Psychologically speaking, mirroring has the effect of making other people feel more comfortable, and it puts them at ease

- ❍ **DO** take the occasional opportunity to let a little of your mischievous personality shine through—a witty aside, a compliment, or wry comment that transcends the business at hand without being too far afield.

- ❍ **DON'T** belly laugh at jokes. Keep it to a delighted laugh instead.

- ❍ **DO** smile and twinkle your eyes to express your fascination with the other person's ideas and insights. Act enthralled!

- ❍ **DON'T** fiddle with your hair. What's sexy in a bar works against you in a boardroom.

- ❍ **DO** share one personal story (within reason) about yourself. Sharing creates intimacy. Encourage the other person to share a story of his own.

- ❍ **DON'T** ignore any sexual chemistry that arises through your business flirtation. If the heat's really on, you'll feel it. Harness that energy and make it work for you, not against you. Above all else, don't cross any lines of propriety.

can also be a great place to meet men—especially men who share the same beliefs and values that you do. While it might seem a bit gauche or forward to boldly flirt in a house of worship, you can use those few minutes either directly before the service or after to chat up anyone who seems interesting enough to you that you might want to get to know them better. Absolutely don't forget to check out the bulletin board. Churches and temples always run socializing activities geared to bring their members closer together. Many of them openly advertise get-togethers for singles.

⤍ DO save the sexy outfits for someplace else. A house of worship is no place for fishnets!

⤍ DON'T sit in the first row. Nobody but the clergy can see you.

⤍ DO speak in a demure, low voice. Raucous laughter is not appropriate.

⤍ DON'T wear a ton of perfume. In a closed space, it can totally overwhelm.

⤍ DO speak to the rabbi, priest, or minister on your way out. It gives any man who wants to talk to you a chance to gather his courage while you're speaking with someone else.

⤍ DON'T head straight for the parking lot after the service. Instead, see if there's some wonderful committee that needs your help.

⤍ DO look a trifle pious—even if you're not!

Is That a Hammer in Your Pocket or Are Ya Just Glad to See Me?

Home improvement stores are great places to flirt. Stores like Lowe's or Home Depot are huge—and there are always lots of guys milling around, making it the perfect location to cruise and schmooze. Okay, so you're an independent woman who can wield a drill with the best of them, but that doesn't mean you can't ask a helpful hunk a question or two about the showerheads, right?

Gallery Openings

Whether you prefer Degas or art deco, gallery openings are classic places to meet and greet. For one thing, you can wear a fabulous outfit and ditch your bar clothes for the evening. The object of the event is to mingle, mingle, mingle. Plus, there is always a bar of some sort. And, of course, the reason you're there in the first place—to look at the art—gives you the perfect excuse to talk to people.

Even if you don't know a thing about art, you can just cock your hip, tilt your head, plaster your face with a thoughtful, pensive expression and say, "Hmm." Other good lines to throw out at a gallery opening are "What do you think of that?" "I wonder how long it took to paint," or "This is really provocative." If you feel like playing the flatterer, you can ask, "Is that your piece?" Often, the Object of Your Flirtation will be so flattered that you mistook him for an artist that he might even take you to dinner. What a bonus!

Political Events

Whether you're Democrat, Republican, Independent, or Green, political events are fabulous fodder for finding good flirts. You don't have to be of the same political persuasion to have a good time.

Basically you have one of two choices for flirting at a political event.

1. You can be a smarty-pants know-it-all who wows all the guys with your intelligent observations and big brain.
2. You can be a political newbie who asks the cutest guy standing next to you to "please explain."

If you are new to the political scene, volunteer for committees or offer to pass around petitions. These are great ways to meet loads of people, not to mention gain brownie points.

As you can see, it's possible to flirt anywhere! Whether you're shopping for food, hanging out in the Laundromat, or simply moseying around a bookstore, just about any location is fertile territory for flirting. Now that you've mastered the art of location, let's move on to the all-important topic of What You Should Wear.

CHAPTER 3

DID YOU SAY **WONDERBRA**?

Always go for the pushup bra.
And make it *demi-décolletage*
while you're at it.

The first step to facile flirting is feeling amazing about yourself. Feel confident and the world is your oyster. All you have to do is go out and get it!

Taking time to groom yourself is critical to optimizing your flirtability potential. This doesn't mean that you have to put on your best clothes and douse yourself with perfume just to walk the dog, but why would you choose to cover yourself in stained, tatty old sweats when you can just as easily outfit yourself in a cute, well-fitting velour hoodie and matching yoga pants? You can meet some of the most adorable guys early in the morning—from your daily coffee hangout to the local dog run.

Another reason for pampering yourself with nice clothes, regular manicures and pedicures, and girly gear like filmy lingerie is that when you feel confident about yourself, you'll be a *much* more confident flirt. You don't have to be a Rhodes scholar to make the connection between your inner self and your outer self. If you don't wake up every morning prepared to maximize your potential, nobody else will see your potential either!

Dale Carnegie, who wrote the most famous self-help book of his time, *How to Win Friends and Influence People,* said that the expression on a woman's face is far more important than the clothes she wears on her back. Okay, so this may be true, but that doesn't mean you shouldn't pay some heed to what you are wearing. If you truly want to elevate yourself to fabulous flirt status, it is *très* important to put some effort into your appearance and state of mind through regular pilgrimages to your favorite lingerie shop, perfume counter, nail and hair salon, shoe boutique, or whatever it is that makes you feel like a queen. This doesn't necessarily mean that you have to go out and blow a week's salary on a complete makeover. Even a once-a-month pampering treat that you can look forward to will work wonders.

> I always feel sexier when I'm wearing
> great lingerie. In fact, I never buy it
> with a man in mind;
> I buy it to please myself!
> —*Suzanne*

No matter what you decide in the exterior beauty department, do be true to your instincts. If you're not feeling comfortable with who you are, how can you feel comfortable with flirtation? Just because you're a cowgirl type who feels most at home in boots and jeans, that doesn't mean you can't make the most of it. Be sure your fanny is cosseted by the very best-fitting jeans you can afford. Don't even think for a minute about buying any pants that don't make your butt look scrumptious!

It's truly amazing how much of a positive impact a little sprucing up on the outside can have. You don't have to decorate the entire tree, just embellish with a few ornaments. You may not have the time or the inclination to go for an entire makeover, but you could take a few minutes to have your eyebrows shaped to make your eyes more beguiling, or pop in for a quick pedicure on your lunch hour.

You might think it's banal or frivolous to claim that your outer trappings have any real effect on your flirtability quotient, but consider the circumstances. You're going to *feel* good if you *look* good, right? Maybe you've just come out of a committed relationship and your wardrobe and hairdo could use a little updating now that you're back "out there." The dating world is a tough place, and you don't want to be out-flirted. When you're out in the marketplace, how you package yourself does count. In your case, a terrific haircut, well-fitting clothes, and a fresh new scent might be all it takes to make you blossom. It's these little accoutrements that will encourage you to strut your stuff, allow you to glow, and help reveal you as the scintillating, sexy, delicious person you really are!

Let's begin with lingerie.

FUN-TO-WEAR UNDERWEAR

Luckily we are living in a time when, rather than being hidden, lingerie is celebrated as a fashion in its own right. Suddenly, lingerie isn't just for under our clothes anymore—wearing a lacy, sexy cami top with your favorite jeans is a perfect way to increase your flirtability, and get in touch with your feminine side.

From small lingerie boutiques to huge chains, sexy underwear is out of the closet, so to speak. Fortunately for you and your credit card, there is a wealth of fabulous underwear to choose from in a range of prices.

Not up on the latest lingerie labels? Here are a few to get you started, from affordable to oh-so-chic:

- Lejaby
- Wacoal
- Felina
- Aubade
- La Perla
- Rampage
- Jezebel

But don't let all of these fancy names fool you—even a department store brand like Maidenform makes beautiful, enticing undergarments.

If you've been a slave to plain old rugged cotton, it's time to change things up! *No* matter what your style, there's something out there for you. From filmy thongs to tap pants, from boy briefs to bikini, try to focus on decadent, sensual fabrics. You'll be thrilled at the way slippery fabrics like satin and silk or even fishnets and lace feel against your skin. And don't worry—you won't be spending your weekend hand-washing your delicates. Just toss them into a net lingerie bag on the delicate cycle, and you're in business. All but the most fragile lingerie can be run through the washing machine.

I like my husband to enjoy folding my underwear when he does the laundry. It's a turn-on for him to handle all my sexy stuff.
—*Linda*

8 GREAT DRESSING TIPS FOR WOMEN
FROM REAL GUYS

1. "Leave an extra button undone on your blouse or shirt. Even if I can't see anything, there's always hope that I will."

   —Doug, 33

2. "The word 'skirt' rhymes with 'flirt.' Skirts are very flirty. Ditto high heels."

   —Josh, 40

3. "Lipstick is a must!"

   —Luis, 30

4. "Turtlenecks can be very sexy, especially on a woman with a long neck."

   —Stephen, 36

5. "I love women who wear cologne—it gives me a chance to strike up a conversation by asking what scent she's wearing."

   —James, 25

6. "I love it when a woman touches me under the pretense of straightening my tie or brushing a piece of lint from my jacket."

   —Keith, 31

7. "If you're showing cleavage, wear a pretty necklace. The jewelry draws my eye to that part of your body. Sweet!"

   —Tom, 38

8. "We love VPL (visible panty line). How come? It reminds us that you are wearing panties, and we just love anything about panties. We just love the 'panty' word."

   —Bob, 30

Asparagus is very sexy. Those long, narrow stalks are the perfect veggie to fiddle with over a romantic meal—and they look so sexy sliding into your mouth. Serve them *al dente* for a bit of crunch.

BUSTIN' OUT

A great bra is a girl's best friend. No other article of clothing can do so much—or so little—for you. That's why it's important to pick your bras carefully. And hopefully get to pick lots and lots of them! Yeah, yeah, you say—I know all about bras. But how much do you really know? Choosing a bra is a serious affair. If you're not comfortable in your bra, you won't be comfortable when you're out there flirting. Now, let's get down to bra business:

Size Matters!

The first challenge in finding the right bra is to figure out your correct size. You'd be amazed to know that the majority of your female counterparts—your friends, your coworkers, your neighbors—are wearing the wrong bra size! It's hard to believe, but if you pulled up the shirts of most adult women you'd find that they're wearing a size they wore in high school or what they wore before childbirth—even if they now have three kids! The average American woman has never had the experience of being properly measured and fitted for a bra. That's why it's so important to go to a *real* lingerie shop, get into that dressing room, and let a professional apply the tape measure!

Once you know your right size, you can really start shopping.

SHOPPING SPREE

So, now you know your size and your style. What should you have in your drawer? Your minimal bra collection should include the following.

⟶ 4 underwire bras

Even if your boobs are pretty tiny, you still want to go for an underwire bra. Even in a 32A cup, an underwire bra will lift your breasts. An underwire demi-bra with even a teeny bit of padding will make your breasts super shapely in a tight T-shirt or tank, or give guys something to peek at near the open throat of your blouse.

⟶ 2 seamless bras for wearing under knits and T-shirts

These are your all-purpose bras that won't show bumps under clingy fabrics. But that doesn't mean you can't have fun with them. Pick out a few in some bright colors that appeal to you.

⟶ 2 to 3 "fun" bras

Fun bras are the ones *not* meant to be worn under clothes. They are the clothes! Victoria's Secret makes lots of bras that are meant for lounging around the house, sort of like sexy pajamas, as well as bras covered in sequins or tons of lace—just to wear in bed with a boyfriend. The thing about bras is once you start collecting them, it can be hard to stop!

---> 1 balcony bra or a great demi-cup number with removable push-up pads

A balcony bra literally turns your breasts into a sexy, gorgeous shelf—a place where males will want to rest their heads, or hang their hat, whatever. If the wide-set straps of a balcony bra don't flatter you (and they might not if you have large shoulders), try a regular half coverage (demi-cup) bra with push-up power to create the same effect.

PANTY PLEASERS AND MORE

Now that you've got the bra thing settled, don't forget the matching panties. Boy cut, briefs, bikini string, even thong—they're all possibilities as long as you're comfortable in them. Remember: Go with whatever style is most suitable for you, but pick a luxurious fabric that will make you feel great. Even if nobody sees you in your skivvies but you, you'll feel more confident about yourself if you're wearing undergarments that make you feel sexy and beautiful.

In addition to your bras and panties, you should have a couple of camisoles, preferably in black, nude, and white. Also, keep several hosiery choices on hand, including at least one pair of fishnets. If you've got long legs, try a garter belt and regular hose, or a pair of sexy black thigh-highs. These are excellent for flashing bits of skin, especially when you're engaging in a flurry of high-stool leg crossing. (More on that later.)

> It's okay to be small.
> I have a tiny cute shape that men seem to enjoy.
> One boyfriend called my underwear
> "doll's clothes." I think he loved that!
> —Lisa

It's very inspirational to pull open your lingerie drawer in the morning and see an inspiring stack of yummy bras and panties waiting for you. Even on rainy, PMS-y, low-energy days, you'll feel more positive and sexy as soon as you get out of the shower and slip into something that is beautiful and fits you like a glove. Remember: Don't scrimp on cheesy underwear. When it comes to lingerie, stick to the good stuff. Cheap underwear just makes a girl feel . . . cheap!

SENSUAL SCENTS

It's been said that of all the six senses, it's smell that stays with us the longest and provokes the most evocative sensations and memories. In the animal kingdom, the sense of smell is integral to the mating ritual, and humans haven't lost that primordial instinct. Smell is a trigger, and that's why it's essential that you regularly anoint yourself with an aroma that makes you feel and smell good.

Aside from the basics of keeping your body clean and fresh, what kind of message do you hope to convey through your perfume? Are you sassy, brazenly sexy, or are you channeling the girl next door? Use the following as a guide to help you figure it all out.

Musky

Musk is associated with original sin—a heady, earthy scent for a very sensual woman. Some people think musk is a real aphrodisiac. Try wearing Kingdom by Alexander McQueen or Obsession by Calvin Klein. Warning: This is very strong stuff!

Sensual

Everyone has her own idea of what sensual is, but Calypso Chevre-feuille by Christiane Celle is a great scent to check out. This French cologne is an alluring floral fragrance that seems light and clean but is laced with a touch of the intoxicating aroma of honeysuckle. It smells somewhat like a slightly alcoholic fruit beverage. Men seem to love it! Also try Stella McCartney's Stella.

Clean

The clean thing is very hot right now. Clean has all the authority of youth and freshness and implies athletic ability. If you think this is the scent for you, sniff some Lauren Style by Ralph Lauren—you'll love it!

Playful

Every girl needs different perfumes to suit her different moods, and playful definitely should be one of them. For a really playful air, try Curious, the perfume designed by Britney Spears.

Classic

A woman can never go wrong with classic scents, much like she can never go wrong with gold hoops or a strand of pearls. Some things never go out of fashion, like Chanel No. 5 or Polo. Spritz yourself with one of these timeless fragrances for a little bit of classic movie star style.

> I am totally into Obsession.
> I've been wearing it forever.
> I always get a lot of compliments
> when I wear it . . . from men and women.
> —*Joann*

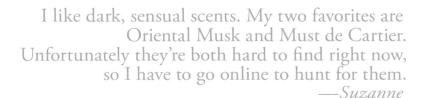

I like dark, sensual scents. My two favorites are Oriental Musk and Must de Cartier. Unfortunately they're both hard to find right now, so I have to go online to hunt for them.
—Suzanne

How to Wear It

Where you choose to put that perfume is just as important as what perfume you choose. Your pulse points are the most obvious locations—that is, on your wrist, at the base of your throat, inside your elbows, behind your knees, and your ankles. If you're not using a heavy scent, try spritzing some in your hair and near your armpits as well for an all-over, lasting scent.

HAIR WE GO—AGAIN!

Hair and makeup are part of your flirt arsenal. Men love hair. So no matter if you've got long, shiny hair, cute and sexy short hair, bouncy hair, curly hair, straight hair, or even a wig, there is a man out there who will be crazy for it. You probably know which style suits you best by now, so work it as best you can. A word to the wise: Avoid using too much product—your hair should be touchable and soft, not lacquered into a helmet!

Certain hairstyles project specific flirt attitudes. For example, long hair piled high on the top of your head not only shows off your earrings, but it also serves to elongate—and expose—your neck. It's an elegant look that says, "I'm a classy woman. Are you classy enough to flirt with me?"

Does your 'do fit your flirt style? The list on page 44 will help you determine what your hair says about you.

EVE'S TIPS . . .

1. Make a point of wearing sexy underwear every day—or no underwear at all.

2. Go lingerie shopping with a friend. A guy friend, that is! He doesn't have to be your lover, although after you rifle through piles of bras and panties together and maybe you model some good stuff, he may very well turn into your lover. . . . If he's a gay guy, make him tell you which sexy underwear does the most for you.

3. Spray yourself with a scent that makes you feel superfeminine and desirable. Right now I'm addicted to Calypso by Christiane Celle. Every time I wear it, men swoon. Once, a virtual stranger was so enamored with the scent, he took a nose-dive into my cleavage. I also love a scent called "Follow Me Boy," which is a combination of essential oils that nineteenth-century courtesans wore to drum up business.

4. Speaking of cleavage, show some. Wear a low-cut silky cami-sole or a V-neck tank top under your suit jacket or other outer top, so it just peeks out and highlights your chest area.

5. This isn't for everybody, but leather is sexy. Leather jeans, leather jacket, leather trench coat. Men seem to love it. Just don't wear all your leather at once unless you want to be mis-taken for a dominatrix.

6. Grow your bangs out just enough so that some hair is always covering one eye. Men seem to like the slight veiled effect,

plus it gives a girl a reason to toss her hair—something the opposite sex seems to find very sexy!

7. Jeans—or any trousers for that matter—are great because they let you sit with your legs apart. Try sitting with one leg up on a chair or a table. There's something about the wide-open position that speaks volumes without you saying even one little word.

8. In the winter, make a point of wearing some kind of fur close to your body. It can be a fur scarf, fur-lined gloves, or a fur muff. The fur is soft and sensual and it might help draw out some of your animal spirit.

9. Cowboy boots make a girl feel brash and bold, not to mention taller! They also correct your posture and make you feel more confident. In fact, they make you feel kick-ass! If cowboy boots are not your thing, figure out another style of boots that give you the same effect. For example, if you've got long, thin legs, go for knee-high boots that draw attention to your racehorse lean thighs and perfectly shaped knees. Or maybe you're more the demure kitten type, and midcalf, heeled boots better fit your style. Just remember, you've got to work those legs. Keep crossing and uncrossing them!

10. Pants and trousers that sit a bit below the waist lengthen the torso and make you appear thinner and trimmer. Also, if you've got a small waist, flaunt it! Always wear a belt.

Ponytail

A simple, girly touch for long hair, a ponytail is a youthful look that is also very sporty. Remember, sporty doesn't equal sloppy. Just because you're sporting your hair in a tail doesn't mean it shouldn't be well-groomed, shiny, and brushed to perfection.

Chignon

Like Chanel No. 5 or any other classic perfume, the chignon is a hairstyle that never goes out of style. A chignon is nothing but a loose bun fixed to sit low on the back of the neck. It's a great office look that goes really well with sweater twin sets and pearls. Men like it because they like to imagine loosening that bun. . . and watching the woman's hair spill sexily down over her neck.

Upsweep

There are all kinds of ways to pile your hair on top of your head. You can have a sexy, rumpled upswept look that is casual and relaxed or a neat, formal "French twist" style that is both elegant and proper. If you have a long neck, this is a great style to show it off. Remember to wear jewelry!

Men always automatically say they love long hair, and long hair is undeniably sexy, but that doesn't mean you can't be sexy with a short haircut. Many men love women with short hair—think of Halle Berry. She proves that short hair can be just as sexy as long hair. Short hair particularly suits petite women, but what it all really comes down to is matching your hair with the attitude you want to project—and have fun with it!

AND NOW FOR SOME MAKEUP

Most men claim to dislike makeup or any cosmetic they deem "artificial." Even the most "fresh as a daisy" women look better with a bit of makeup, even if it's only bronzer or a touch of mascara. And as for lipstick, remember this simple rule: A little lipstick goes a long way. Most guys find it sexy to watch a woman apply lipstick.

How much time should you spend on your hair and makeup if you want to feel flirty and sexy? That's really up to you. Many girls never leave the house without putting on a full array of makeup, while others think nothing of dashing out for the day with their faces bare and naked to the world. By the same token, many women are slavish about spending an hour with their trusty blow dryer, while others have no difficulty hopping straight from the shower and heading off to the office with a wet head. As long as you're feeling flirty and fabulous, stick with what works for you.

Quick Makeup Tricks

Unless you are moonlighting as a Kabuki performer, the purpose of makeup is not to create a mask. Use makeup to enhance your best features. Aside from the occasional blemish, your goal is to draw attention to something, not hide it. Again, it's the "Work with what you have" rule.

Do you have fantastic eyes? Always wear mascara! Full, pouting lips? Go for the lip gloss. Are your cheekbones prominent and chiseled? Draw attention to them by hitting them with a brush of bronzer.

Don't be afraid of foundation makeup. It does wonders for evening out skin tones. If you're afraid of wearing anything that may be too powdery or too deep-concealing, try a tinted moisturizer. Go to a makeup counter at any good department store. Better yet, go to Sephora, the makeup, skin care, fragrance, bath and body, and hair giant that lets you

sample just about every great brand of makeup. Their salespeople are trained to help you find what looks best on you and to teach you about (and how to use) all the latest products.

THEY DON'T CALL THEM EFF-ME PUMPS FOR NOTHING

It has been said that the right shoes can make or break an image. Okay, so this might be a little overkill, but the right pair of shoes can make you feel more flirtatious than ever, whether you're strapped into your spikiest Manolo Blahniks or taking it easy in espadrilles.

I have to have high heels. I just don't feel like my true sexy self can come through wearing flats.
—Colleen

Susan Reynolds, author of *Change Your Shoes, Change Your Life,* devotes an entire chapter to the topic of shoes and sex. She says, "As the Cinderella myth belies, shoes have always been an important ingredient in sex appeal. Men find any extremely feminine shoes romantic, but they adore high heels. From mules that expose luscious legs and feet to thigh-high boots that stop just short of her 'garden,' high heels pitch a woman's body forward and put a sway in her hips that men find devastatingly alluring." Because she says she finds it difficult to wear high heels anymore, she looks for sexy low-heeled rhinestone sandals or brocade pumps trimmed with lace or adorned with a flowered clip; pretty shoes that she feels induce men to notice her femininity and which seem to "work magic."

Every flirt should have an arsenal of essential shoes in her closet. What's in yours?

Boots

A girl can't have too many boots. There are so many styles to choose from! Low-heeled boots are a great casual look to wear with jeans during the day, and tall, high-heeled boots turn jeans into sexy evening wear. Short leather boots are a good business look as an alternative to a classic pump style. Cowboy boots suggest a rough and ready spirit. Over the knee boots scream "sexy!"

Strappy Sandals

Every woman needs one pair of strappy sandals. They can be a delicate formal shoe or sturdy gladiator footwear. Is it the straps that subtly suggest the look of bondage? Maybe that's why most men find them so sexy.

Flats

While most men say they prefer a woman in heels, flats are flirty because they mean you can move quickly. Also if you're fairly tall, flats are essential to keep you from towering over some men. (If you're really tall, play it up by wearing the highest heels you can find. You will look awesome!)

Q At 3:30, I'm meeting a guy I've been flirting with online for four weeks now. He's on his way to a meeting and will be in a suit. What should I wear?

A Dress to his level as much as possible. In other words, dress pretty nice. It may be totally freezing, but does he warrant a skirt? Something that shows your knees?

Q What shoes should I wear with it?

A If you have high boots, wear them. Whenever possible, show your knees. Knees are like breasts on your legs. Men always look at them.

I love wearing hot shoes, especially pumps or sexy sandals that have slim, high heels. I also love anything with slim ankle straps. That makes me feel sexy and in the mood to flirt with my feet!
—Suzanne

Sneakers, Hiking Boots, and More

Every woman needs an action shoe if she expects to get any action. A pair of hiking boots coupled with short shorts shows off your legs, and the bulky boots also serve to make your legs look slimmer and longer. This "rough and ready" look signals to a guy, "Hey, I'm in great shape," and here is just a preview of what kind of workout you might be getting in the future if you play your cards right!

DRESS ME UP, DRESS ME DOWN!

What you wear on the rest of your body also sets a mood for how you feel about yourself. If you're into flirty dresses, why not add a few more to your wardrobe?

Look for clothes that flatter your body type and that help you feel confident and at ease. For example, a skin-tight sweater or a low-cut blouse might make you look supersexy to men, but if you have large breasts that you're not entirely comfortable with, you won't ever feel hot in that top. Go for something less obvious that shows off your figure without exploiting it, like a well-fitting cashmere crewneck.

Flirt Skirts

Men love women in skirts. Skirts can be tricky, though. What length you choose depends on the shape of your legs and where you are going. Really short skirts are never appropriate at the office! Most women look good with a skirt that hits them an inch or two above the knee. A casual skirt worn in a casual setting is fine sans stockings. Always wear hose for formal occasions and usually in the office.

Trousers

Katharine Hepburn was the first American woman to always wear pants. She said she had "very sharp knees" that she preferred to keep covered up, and since she was an avid sportswoman, pants suited her lifestyle. Today many women wear pants 90 percent of the time. There are a dozen styles of trousers out there, everything from skinny cigarette pants to wide-legged trousers to casual khakis to business pantsuits. The only thing that matters is that yours fit well. When in doubt, ask a friend to tell you if they truly flatter your front and rear view.

CHAPTER 4

DAILY FLIRTING

Remember that old adage,
an apple a day? A *flirt* a *day*
will keep you *much* healthier!

A girl should flirt at least once every day. Actually, ten or fifteen times a day is more like it, unless you've been knocked flat by the flu—and even then you can find an opportunity or two to flirt.

As we already covered in Chapter 2, there are flirting opportunities galore flashing right in front of you that you may have been oblivious to before you read this book. To flirt well, you have to be totally aware of others and your surroundings. You can't expect to flirt well if you spend all of your time with your cell glued to your ear, or e-mailing from your BlackBerry. Look around. Everything is raw material. Take the cute guy working at the Shell station who looks like Clive Owen. Sexy! Now that's a prime Flirt Object! So, why, oh why would you pump your own gas when a handsome and flirtable man is being paid to pump it for you? This is just one of many opportunities you could be taking advantage of!

There are twenty-four hours in a day and you could be spending more of them flirting.

THE 24-HOUR FLIRT SCHEDULE

To help you figure out how to incorporate flirting into your daily repertoire, you can use the 24-Hour Flirt Schedule.

Actually, it helps to break it down even further than that. Think of flirting in minutes. Moments. Nanoseconds, even. Some of the best flirts last no longer than butterfly kisses. Besides, it's unreasonable to expect every flirtation to be a marathon. Marathons are a lot of work! Of course, there will be times when you will be flirting for hours, and that will be enjoyable, too. The 24-Hour Flirt Schedule will help you make the most of each flirty moment—from morning until night.

Even if you work in retail or in a bank or an office, even if you're a bicycle messenger (what an amazing job—imagine the people you might meet, not to mention the glute workout), even if you punch a time clock, there are myriad opportunities to flirt throughout the day. Let's see. There's the elevator operator, the guy at the lobby newsstand, the coffee cart guy, the guy sitting in the next cubicle, the mailroom guy, cab drivers, horse-drawn carriage operators, doormen, your boss?

Depending on your job, you may have more or less flirting opportunities, but they *are* out there. (And okay, it is a challenge to find people to flirt with if you're a nanny with triplets on your hands, but have you really looked around your neighborhood playground lately?) You just need to pay attention, and look at your surroundings with new eyes. If every day you manage to initiate even two or three flirtations, I promise that you will see a rapid overall improvement of your flirting skills. So get started! Ladies . . . start flirting!

The following is a sample of Lisa's 24-Hour Flirting Schedule.

LISA'S 24-HOUR **FLIRT** SCHEDULE

⏰ 7:00 A.M.—Clock goes off. Before even stepping out of bed, Lisa stretches, looks up at the ceiling, and repeats her flirting mantra five times: "Today is going to be my best flirt day ever. It will be a good flirting day, a great flirting day, an excellent flirting day, the best!"

⏰ 7:05 A.M.—She hops into the shower, lathers up with her favorite products, and gets in touch with her inner flirt by making sure she starts off the day feeling fabulous.

⏰ 7:22 A.M.—Lisa buffs herself all over with a nice soft fluffy towel. Peach is a good color—always flattering. Next she slathers on her favorite lotion: moisturize, moisturize, moisturize! When it comes to moisture, a girl can never get enough. Besides, even Lisa can't know when a sexy someone might happen to brush up against her. She wouldn't want to scare him off with alligator skin, would she?

⏰ 7:30 A.M.—Lisa generously spritzes herself with her favorite cologne. Scent, as she knows, is a major tool for flirting! Lisa expertly applies her mascara and lipstick, and dots her cheeks with blush. Work is war. A girl needs war paint.

⏰ 8:00 A.M.—Consider the day's flirt uniform, oops, outfit. Will it be the short skirt with the patterned hose or the fitted side-zip pants? The soft cardigan with the top button undone or a semisheer blouse? Strappy sandals or boots? And what to wear beneath it all? Thong or no thong? (Even if Lisa has spent her whole life hating it, men love Visible Panty Line!)

⏰ **8:48 A.M.**—Lisa rides up the elevator with a really cute guy. She casts a good sidelong look at him. She waits a beat while he takes it in, then gives him another look, this time with her eyebrows raised. Lisa smiles winningly at him when she gets to her floor. She says, "Ta-ta! Have a nice day," before she sashays out the door.

⏰ **9:00 A.M.**—Getting to her desk, Lisa bends over, waaaay over, when she slips her bag into her desk drawer. It's okay because she's wearing trousers at the office. As she stands back up, she notices one of her male coworkers staring. She grins and gives her trademark nod before settling into her seat.

⏰ **10:15 A.M.**—Lisa flashes some pearly whites at the office intern whose job it is to bring all those dull files to her. Even if he's much too young and still has a face covered in zits, she makes his day by finding a charming word for him.

⏰ **10:30 A.M.**—Lisa tries not to be the first one to leap out of her seat at the sound of the coffee cart. She waits for that cute guy in the opposite cubicle (the one who enjoyed studying her ass earlier) to offer to get her something. She thanks him as she reaches for her purse, and acts totally surprised and charmed when he says, "Hey, it's on me."

⏰ **12:30 P.M.**—Lisa blows a kiss to her boss as she heads off for lunch. Even though her boss is a woman.

⏰ **12:32 P.M.**—No one interesting to flirt with in the elevator on the way down, but Lisa knows that lunch hour is a prime flirtation time.

FLIRTATIOUS
LIBATIONS

Sex and the City may have started it, but as a flirtastic woman, you would be remiss if you didn't sip this cocktail every once in a while. Here's a quick recipe:

The Flirtini
1 ounce vodka
2 ounces champagne
2 ounces pineapple juice

1. Combine the vodka, champagne, and pineapple juice in a highball or Collins glass filled with ice. For a party or multiple servings, multiply the recipe and mix in a pitcher.

2. Variations on the recipe: Add ½ ounce of Cointreau or add fresh pineapple slices or a cherry garnish. Feel free to mess around with the combinations. Just as there is no one right way to flirt, there's no one right way to mix up a Flirtini!

⏰ 12:45 P.M.—As she's doing some shopping at the department store, she happens upon a hunky guy in the men's cologne department. He looks lost, so she critiques his scent and helps him pick one that suits him. She leaves with his number.

⏰ 1:00 P.M.—On her way back to the office, Lisa grabs an ice cream sundae—after all, every girl deserves a treat, and ice cream is a very flirty dessert!

⏰ 1:15 P.M. TO 3:15 P.M.—Lisa works at looking superindustrious and totally engrossed in her work. Doesn't give office "frenemies" the time of day. At the same time, she keeps one eye peeled on the water cooler and manages to be parched with thirst if anyone she deems adorable heads that way.

⏰ 3:17 P.M.—Lisa sneaks in a personal phone call to her best friend to discuss her evening agenda. Even though she's only talking about what she plans to watch on TV, she chuckles in her lowest, throatiest voice when any fascinating gents stroll by.

⏰ 4:20 P.M.—She draws up a brilliant memo detailing her next great self-directed work plan for earning the company pots and pots of money. She presents it to her superior and smiles knowingly when she exclaims, "This is genius!"

⏰ 5:15 P.M.—Quitting time! (Lisa always stays an extra fifteen minutes to impress her boss with how industrious and committed she is.) She does that bend-over thing again when retrieving her purse. She acts really pleased and surprised when the guy in the next cubicle asks if she's got time for a drink. Lisa says, "No thank you," very sweetly. Sure, he's cute, but she would never get involved in an office romance—strictly against the rules!

⏰ **6:05 P.M. TO 6:59 P.M.**—Lisa lolls in her bathtub reading her favorite celebrity gossip magazines. She does not bother with the New Republic since she's not going anywhere where she'll be required to chat up left-wing intellectuals. She sticks with publications detailing celebrity break-ups. As she relaxes in her bubbles and closes her eyes, she imagines all the great repartee and clever things she would say if only she could get next to these celebs.

⏰ **7:00 P.M.**—Lisa rises from the tub. She envisions herself as a mermaid-like goddess emerging from the ocean. She channels Venus on the Half Shell, and ignores the reality that her clam is really a tatty old bath mat.

⏰ **7:25 P.M.**—Lisa stands in front of her armoire and surveys her wardrobe. She's headed out for a gala night on the town. . . . Okay, it's really just the corner pub. She selects an appropriate outfit that best shows off just enough cleavage. Her secret: She really has no cleavage, and she puts on a push-up bra for added effect.

⏰ **8:00 P.M.**—Lisa shakes her booty for a few minutes in front of her full-length mirror. Practices wiggling her hips. She sings a few bars of "You Sexy Thing," for confidence.

⏰ **8:45 P.M.**—Lisa sails out the door in a cloud of sweet perfume.

⏰ **8:47 P.M.**—Minor setback. Lisa's friend and regular bar-hopping buddy calls to bail because she's spending an intimate evening a deux with her new beau, pizza, and a DVD. Lisa does not become disheartened or dismayed, or even a little frustrated. Even though she's been single three years and nary a decent man (forget about white knights) has yet to loom on her horizon, she tells herself that the stars are all aligned and tonight's her lucky night. Bagging a good guy is a lot like winning the lottery. You've got to be in it to win it.

⏰ **9:17 P.M.**—Lisa saunters into the bar and acts like she owns the joint.

⏰ **9:20 P.M.**—She turns down the first offer she gets from a guy hoping to buy her a drink. Note: A good flirt always turns down the first drink offer.

⏰ **9:30 P.M.**—While scoping out the possibilities and enjoying her drink, Lisa commences a light flirtation with the bartender, who's definitely a cutie.

⏰ **9:40 P.M.**—Lisa is wondering whether or not to declare it an unflirtatious night when the bartender informs her that a hot prospect is headed in her direction. She tries not to look too interested.

⏰ **9:41 P.M.**—She can't avoid looking deeply annoyed when it turns out that the "hot prospect" is her ex.

⏰ **9:42 P.M.**—Lisa resists the urge to scream, "What the hell are you doing here?" She smiles sweetly at him and permits Mr. Ex to buy her a drink. He owes her at least that much, right?

🕐 **10:00 P.M.**—As soon as she finishes her drink, she glances at her watch, and says, "I'm sorry, but you'll have to go. I'm waiting for Prince Charming."

🕐 **10:05 P.M.**—In an effort to get rid of him, Lisa uses a little bit of sexy three-party flirting to introduce him to the attractive woman sitting nearby. (Note: You'll learn more about three-party flirting very soon!) She decides that if she's going to have a decent flirtation of her own tonight, she needs to be her ex's ally, not his enemy. At least for now. The sooner she gets him engaged in flirting with somebody else, the sooner she can concentrate on her own flirt target.

🕐 **10:20 P.M.**—Lisa switches to Perrier, politely turning down the bartender's offer of buybacks for the next round. She knows the rules. No matter how good you're feeling at the moment, remember that there's nothing really attractive about a flirtatious drunk.

🕐 **10:30 P.M.**—When Lisa finally sees someone worth flirting with, she works it. Tosses her hair. Stares into his eyes. Lowers her chin. Crosses her legs. Twirls her swizzle stick and wraps her fingers around the stem of her wineglass. Touches his arm. Laughs. Tells a joke. The moment she's got her quarry totally captivated, she announces she must leave.

🕐 **10:35 P.M.**—Lisa swings her backside off that barstool and heads for the door. Nice girls never linger at the bar alone for more than an hour. Her time is up!

🕐 **11:00 P.M.**—At home at her computer, Lisa checks her e-mail one more time. She dashes off a cute reply to the Blueyedtxcwby who wants to know her bra size. She tells him anything she pleases since she knows she'll probably never meet him. He's the best kind of flirt of all. A cyberguy.

11:12 P.M.—Lisa washes her face, brushes her teeth, and applies moisturizer. She pastes Crest White Strips to her teeth to enhance her smile. She remembers that a beautiful smile is a flirty girl's best friend!

11:30 P.M.—Lisa slips under the covers for well-deserved beauty rest. As she pulls her pink velvet sleep mask down over her face, she whispers to herself her special mantra, "I am the flirt queen."

As you can see, Lisa's day isn't so much about following a flirt schedule as it is about making the most of every opportunity and working her flirt charms to the best of her abilities. If you're wondering how to put a little more flirt into your life, why not quickly jot down your own 24-Hour Flirt Schedule? Your path to the ultimate flirtation should be filled with good intentions—and lots of fun! It's like multitasking for the Flirting Inclined.

YOUR 24-HOUR **FLIRT** SCHEDULE

⏰ 7:00 A.M.	
⏰ 8:00 A.M.	
⏰ 9:00 A.M.	
⏰ 10:00 A.M.	
⏰ 11:00 A.M.	
⏰ 12:00 P.M.	
⏰ 1:00 P.M.	
⏰ 2:00 P.M.	
⏰ 3:00 P.M.	
⏰ 4:00 P.M.	
⏰ 5:00 P.M.	
⏰ 6:00 P.M.	
⏰ 7:00 P.M.	
⏰ 8:00 P.M.	
⏰ 9:00 P.M.	
⏰ 10:00 P.M.	
⏰ 11:00 P.M.	
⏰ 12:00 A.M.	

CHAPTER 5

KUNDALINA, SPAGHETTINI, OUI OUI, OLÉ
(IT'S NOT WHAT YOU SAY, IT'S HOW YOU SAY IT)

Speak a little *French*.
Look at the effect it had on
Gomez when Morticia spoke it
on *The Addams Family*.

There are many first-rate flirters out there who almost never rely on body language to get their flirt across, at least not initially. (Later, when they've stunned their quarry into a state of hopeless infatuation, they move in for the kill by deploying arm stroking and leg weapons.)

Verbal flirtation is an excellent way to hone your flirting skills, but it's not for the faint of heart! Verbal flirters tend to be highly intelligent individuals who excel at games like Scrabble. They're quick on their feet, so to speak. They're experts at wordplay and fun verbal sparring. They are charming, and they know how to get and maintain a captive audience by making their quarry feel extra special. Verbal flirters tend to have a great sense of humor, and they're spectacular storytellers.

That said, you don't have to be a linguistic genius who got a perfect verbal score on your SATs to excel at verbal flirtation. It's pretty easy to cultivate an arsenal of verbal gambits that will immediately boost your flirt repertoire. This chapter will help you hone your verbal flirting skills in any situation.

> "I've used simple, obvious questions that work to get someone's attention, like 'Got a light?' or 'Do you have the time?' Corny as this may sound, smiling with my eyes while saying just about anything is a sure way to send a friendly vibe."
> —*Eileen*

FLIRTSPEAK: MASTERING THE LANGUAGE

Flirtspeak is a language all its own, and once you understand it, it's a lot of fun to use! Flirtspeak is really all about subtext.

If you're up for it, this kind of exchange is a great way to get things started, and it goes *waaay* beyond the traditional coy hair-tossing, leg-crossing techniques into unfettered, open flirtation. The woman who is quick on the draw with snappy rejoinders is in for a hot flirt-match, indeed.

Amazing Opening Lines

Opening a conversation with something outrageous can lead to a great flirt.

A good opening line is like gold. Entire books and Web sites devoted to relationship stuff and dating have been dedicated to great opening one-liners. A good opening line opens the door. It gets you inside, and it propels you into action. Having a stellar first line can turn a few-second encounter into a developing relationship.

You don't have to be a genius to come up with good opening lines. In fact, there's very little need to come up with anything original at all! Many of the best ones have been stolen from somebody else. The best ones are classic lines that have been used over and over. Take it from these Certified Flirtation Experts:

It's Cute to Be a Marble Mouth

You're probably asking, "What the heck's a marble mouth?"

This is garbled talk, or tripping over your own words so that they are basically unintelligible. You don't usually do it on purpose. It comes out of nervousness or being so excited that your words get mixed up.

Okay, so it doesn't *sound* especially cute. But it is! Scrambling your words is actually an excellent linguistic flirtation device. In fact, go ahead and mangle them. Remember how adorable Eliza Doolittle was in that scene in *My Fair Lady* when the doctor of linguistics puts all those marbles in her mouth? It was

Now it's time to put your skills to the test. Is the following line flirtspeak or just regular, banal conversational intercourse?

"I'll have a Sex on the Beach, please."

If you answered "flirtspeak," then you go immediately to the head of the class! As everyone knows, anytime a woman utters the words "Sex on the Beach," in any situation or context, it is absolutely, positively, overwhelmingly flirtatious. If you answered "regular conversation," have no fear! This chapter is designed especially to help bring out the best of your verbal flirtation abilities.

To me the best pick-up line is not a pick-up line. It has to seem natural, honest.
—*Lorna*

her charmingly skewed rendering of simple words and sentences that captured and captivated the old bastard. Not to mention it was sexy seeing all that stuff crammed into her mouth. Of course, in her case, a mouthful of marbles and mangled words was a by-product of a dubious pseudoscientific procedure. In your case, however, a well-placed malapropism may be enough. And don't stop with *My Fair Lady*—many, many movies have wonderful verbal flirting scenes—study them as part of your rigorous flirt education curriculum.

"My *marble mouth* usually happens when I become aware that a man is attracted to me. Within a nanosecond of *'Omigod, he's interested!'* it's like the mangling begins! After I've made a *mishmash* out of a simple word or phrase, then the cute factor kicks in.

The guy *smiles* at my mistake, maybe I make another, and poof, pow, a *full flirting moment* has happened."

—Eileen

The Old Double-Entendre

Another linguistic tool you should have at your fingertips is a decent mastery of the double-entendre. A double-entendre is a word or expression that can have two interpretations, with one of them being a bit risqué. It's a French term, and one that should most definitely be part of your flirt vocabulary!

Risqué Business

If you're good at verbal sparring, then you can make the double-entendre work for you. This is a very sexy technique, so proceed with caution. Some obvious examples of double-entendres are "How does this thing go in?" "Where would you like that?" and "I'm ready."

Of course, there's no better way to give you an example of a double-entendre than using a fun film flirt. In the movie *Sideways,* Thomas Haden Church enters into an exchange with his soon-to-be love interest, played by Sandra Oh. After a brief volley of clever and edgy repartee, he says something like, "I can tell, Stephanie, that you're a bad, bad girl." Stephanie's response is, "Yes, I could use a good spanking." Here you have a prime example of a blatant, sexy flirt! But the subtext of this conversation is what's really interesting. The subtext indicates that the guy is really saying, "I appreciate a woman who can be a little bit wild," and her response is saying, "I am that wild child."

This kind of exchange is a great way to get things started, and it can be much more enjoyable than using just body language to flirt. Work on coming up with a couple of snappy rejoinders like this for your flirtation arsenal, and you're sure to have some real fun!

> "When I'm at work and the UPS guy comes to the door, I'll shout, 'Hey Brown, what are you going to do for me today?'"
> —*Eileen*

Jeune Fille

If your approach is more innocent than bold, then the *jeune fille* approach (French for "young, innocent girl") might be a better tactic for you. The best way to deliver this kind of double-entendre is to couple your line with a soupçon of body language, which could be something as subtle as a raised eyebrow or a *Mona Lisa* smile. A *Mona Lisa* smile, by the way, is incredibly flirtatious. The mystery of *Mona Lisa*'s famous smirk is what makes it so flirtatious. So if you're playing the *jeune fille* for the night, work that mysterious smile, baby!

You can also mix and match your flirtation techniques. Just because you're playing the innocent one doesn't mean you can't get a little sexy. Sometimes just delivering a double-entendre line like, "Yeah, you're in," deadpan, works best of all. It makes you appear so naive, so *jeune fille*, which is a hugely popular flirt style.

Who Do You Think You Are . . . Me?

Another useful flirting trick is to use something called *pattern recognition*. Sounds kind of scientific, doesn't it? Don't worry! It's simple. All you have to do is mimic what the other person is saying and how he's saying it. For example, if you're with a guy who has a bit of a Southern accent, slip a few "y'all's" into your conversation.

Or maybe you find yourself chatting with someone who has a cute verbal tic, like he keeps repeating the word "actually." In that situation, pick up his tic and sprinkle your sentences liberally with the very same word. He won't even realize you're playing with his word. What he will notice is that you've got similar speech patterns and that will instantly lull him into feeling more comfortable and relaxed around you! Therapists do this sort of thing all the time. In fact, repeating back exactly what the client says is a bona fide therapeutic technique.

Word to the wise: Don't do this if you've got a thick accent of your own (think Boston or Brooklyn here). If you've got an accent that's unique, don't hold back: Work it! Let your regional accent and locutions act as a conversational gambit, something of its own to talk about.

LIGHTS! ACTION! CAMERA!

YOU'RE AN ACTRESS: ASSUME YOUR ROLE

A little acting never hurt anyone! Next time you're out and about, why not try playing around with your flirtspeak the way an actress takes on different personas.

If you're feeling like you'd like to step outside of your own fabulous starring role, maybe try one of these fun characters on for size:

- **THE WILD CHILD**—She is a free spirit. Her conversation is unfettered and natural, but a bit dangerous. When you're talking with her, you don't know what to expect. Everything and anything will come out of her mouth!

- **THE PREPPY CHICK**—This woman has a bit of locutional lockjaw. She enunciates carefully. But because the Preppy Chick tends to be sporty, her language can be pretty salty. When she wants, this gal can swear like a sailor.

- **THE DEBUTANTE**—She is a true society girl and her speech patterns reflect that. Debs tend to use very high-flown vernacular, when they're not drunk and dancing on tabletops!

- **THE STARLET**—Starlets don't have much to say, but when they do speak at all, it's usually from a rehearsed speech cut down for sound bites. If you're doing Starlet, just smile a lot and pretend you're looking into a camera, and lay on your best one-liners.

- **THE TOMBOY**—She is cute and kind of boyish. Speechwise, she can seem awkward. She's shy and doesn't have much to say. Instead of real language, she points. When she does say something, she's prone to somewhat inappropriate blurting. Usually Tomboys are good-natured. They rely on laughter rather than talking.

Just like you play with different outfits, you can make use of different catch phrases, dialogue, and idioms to create different flirt personas. Just decide on the image you want to project and then sprinkle your dialogue with the corresponding vocabulary, and you're good to go!

Funny Girl

Another verbal flirtation device is to become a great joke teller. Funny girls get a lot of play. Wit is a characteristic highly prized by smart men. You don't have to be a standup comedienne to be funny. Memorize a couple of good jokes (cultivate a revolving repertoire so you're not telling the same jokes all the time) and you'll have guys eating out of your hand. Telling a joke well is a way of captivating an entire audience. It's really a great way to get attention focused on you when you're part of a crowd, in situations like after-work drinks with coworkers and such. Besides, getting to know a guy better is a piece of cake if you can make him laugh.

Condolence Flirting

On the flip side of joke telling, believe it or not, there is such a thing as condolence flirting. There's an urban flirtation legend about a woman who once flirted with an undertaker—though this hasn't been confirmed! This type of flirting is very tricky, though. You're dealing with a person who is grieving in some way, so you absolutely positively *must* come across as sincere.

The cause of the person's grief can't be too grave, either. Don't try flirting up a guy who just learned his mother died; that's just wrong. Very wrong! But if he tells you that he recently lost his favorite goldfish, you have a green light to condolence flirt. Better yet, if he tells you that the reason he's at the bar getting lit is because his crazy girlfriend just kicked him out of the house, you're in like Flint. Or, if he just found out he blew the exam that would admit him to law school or he's feeling a bit blue because he didn't get a big Christmas bonus—well, flirt away, cowgirl!

Tips for condolence flirting: Keep your voice soft and sympathetic.

Choose your words wisely, and be as kind as possible. Depending on the situation, offer a shoulder to cry on—as long as you don't mind the guy getting his face that close to your breast!

Un-Flirting

Sometimes the best flirtatious line is to claim a complete inability to be flirtatious. Try it. It works every time.

> *What I have noticed is that if I say, "Oh geesh, I am a total dork when it comes to flirting," men fall all over themselves.*
> *—Roxanne*

It works because men are pretty gullible. They actually believe (at least in the beginning) almost anything a woman says! Also, since so many men are real players, they're naturally suspicious of women they suspect might be playing *them*. So even if you are an accomplished flirt of the first order, simply telling a man that you aren't flirting with him because you don't know how to flirt gets him excited. What it tells him is that he can get one over on you. Ha, ha! Guess who's foolin' who?

Online Flirting

Online flirting relies, of course, solely on the written word rather than the verbal. As anyone who has spent an evening IMing knows, those words can become very flirtatious! A lot of people love doing all their flirting online, and why not? You're completely incognito. You can hide behind a screen name. You can lie like a rug if you feel like it. No one can see your face, your bod, the fact that you haven't washed your hair in sixteen days. Online you are free as a bird. You can say whatever you want

Flirtatious Gambits to Suss Him Out

It's entirely possible to flirt with a man for the purpose of gleaning Important Information. Specifically: Is he available or not? Here's some lines you can try using to suss him out, but remember, flirtatious guys are wily foxes!

"You sound like you spend a lot of time skiing. Does your wife ski, too?"

"It's so cool that we just saw the same concert. Who'd you go with?"

"Is that a bra in your laundry basket? It's so sweet of you to do your sister's wash."

"Hey! I just went to my high school reunion, too. Did you go with anyone?"

"It's so cute to see a big guy with a tiny white dog. That is your dog, isn't it?"

"I couldn't help noticing that you're not wearing a wedding band."

(as long as you don't start spewing obscene expletives, which will get you kicked off). Are you the kind of gal who doesn't really come to life until after midnight? Modern technology has made it so you don't have to leave the house, heck, even get dressed, to exercise your flirt muscles!

There are a few rules regarding online flirting that you should follow if you plan to succeed.

1. Become familiar with your computer's various icons, like those awful smiley face things. But try not to overuse them. Remember, you should be able to flirt using words—not computer icons!

2. Add some of the basic lingo to your vocabulary: LOL means "laugh out loud." BRB means "be right back," which is useful if you have to make a bathroom run, or a pit stop at your refrigerator.

3. Get used to E-breviations. Online flirters also tend to use abbreviated spelling and shorthand writing (the same is true if you're flirting by text message on your cell phone). For example, u is "you," and ttyl means "talk to you later."

Sometimes the Best Flirt Is the One Who Says Nothing at All

A simple yet powerful verbal technique is to just keep on saying "no." If you employ this tactic, you are an elusive and fascinating breed of flirt known as the Refusal Flirt. You're a back-to-basics kind of girl. You're a whiz at playing hard to get. You know you can pull off the princess act, because you're a princess, dammit!

Just saying "no" is a controlling technique (back to those ABCs of Flirting again: remember Approach/Behavior/Control?) that can only be successfully pulled off if:

A. You're supermodel beautiful

> or

B. You handle yourself with supermodel attitude

But even if you're an easygoing, always agreeable, "yes" type of gal, saying "no" once in a while can be a rush. Think of it as a way to exercise your little-used no muscle. There is a highly desirable and select population of flirtatious guys out there who love nothing more than a challenge. A confident, beautiful woman who refuses to settle for the usual verbal gambits represents a mountain to climb, a vista to conquer, new territory to be explored. Engage his attention with an initial refusal to play along and you might just find yourself in for an interesting flirtation that goes way beyond the norm.

> "I told my best flirt friend 'I love you,' about six weeks ago and I haven't heard from him since. My advice to any woman is, avoid those words."
> —*Roxanne*

GLIBIDO AND GLIBIDIOTS

Everyone knows someone who is a total flirt who is "all talk and no action." A person suffering from "glibido" (thank you, *Washington Post*'s Style Invitational) are usually razor-sharp flirts who can flirt up cats, dogs, men, women, basically anything that's breathing. Some of the best flirts in this category are married flirts who have no intention of actually "being with" anyone but enjoy flirting for flirt's sake.

One of the most common types in this category is a very married (as in he's got three kids married) man. Sure, he flirts you up, but he can never take it anywhere else. Another notorious man suffering from glibido is the Ambivalent Guy—the one who's deathly afraid to commit to anything, even a brand of toothpaste. This guy seems like he's great fun at first, and he hints at wanting to see more of you, but then he slips off into the crowd and you never see him again. Either that, or he asks for your number and never calls. Talk about all talk and no action!

Following are some common glibido traits and characteristics:

He seems magnanimous, and he is always armed with ready quips. He can make a pun or a joke out of anything.

He's got a big ego and it shows.

He's usually a good dresser.

He's urbane, suave. You're wondering, "Is he gay?"

He's got smooth moves—too smooth. He fetches you a fresh drink before you even knew yours was empty, and he drops pick-up lines on you that are over the top.

He's bold and confident. Warning! He can be very sexually aggressive!

The Glibidiot

Where glibidos are suave and sexy, glibidiots are not quite as well spoken. Unfortunately, this is one of the hazards of flirting with the same guy for an extended period of time—if you run into a glibidiot, he may get too attached to you too quickly, in a puppy-love sort of way. You know you've had a run-in with a glibidiot if he keeps blurting out *very* wrong things at *very* wrong moments. He usually jumps that border from healthy, innocent exchange right over to expressing his achingly painful crush on you with record speed. Sure, sometimes it's cute. In more extreme cases, it makes for an incredibly uncomfortable situation.

Under certain circumstances (usually ones fueled by alcohol) the glibidiot is likely to say some (or all) of the following:

> *"Oh, I'm so sorry! I didn't mean to spill on you!"*
>
> *"Would you marry me . . . tonight?"*
>
> *"I'm very attracted to you. So is my girlfriend."*
>
> *"I just can't stop staring at your breasts. Are they real?"*

Hair, which every flirt-worthy woman knows how to shake and toss, is made of cuticle, and cuticle is enhanced by the taking of Vitamin B. So if your hair is looking a little dull, try to work some more Vitamin B into your diet. For a glossy head of hair, try eating:

- Bananas
- Spinach
- Fish and poultry

"I love you."

Ugh. These are the three words no respectable flirt should ever say. It's the line that always stops any fun flirting action cold!

In the movies, flirts can get away with saying stuff like that and the camera just moves in on the couple as they fall into each other's arms. In real life, it never works that way and all that's happened is that you've upset or embarrassed the other person.

It's perfectly permissible for him to use "love" about something *related* to you—"I love your eyes," "I love your shoes," even "I love your smile." But when he starts expressing his love for you and you've known him for forty-five minutes, it's time for you to make a quick (albeit flirtatious) getaway.

5 THINGS YOU SHOULD
NEVER SAY

There are certain things you should never say to a man—unless you want to send a clear and final message that you wish he would get lost. Here's some verbiage you can use to blow off any relatively normal, sane guy. Note: If you happen to come across a guy who is turned on by these words, run, run, *run* for the hills!

1. "Yes, I'm married. To a very jealous man."

2. "I live with my mother . . . and her mother, too."

3. "I've got three kids under the age of five. You like kids, don't you?"

4. "This sore on my lip? Oh, it's just a mild case of herpes. Don't give it a second thought."

5. "That's so sweet of you to get me another drink. Make mine a ginger ale. I just found out I'm pregnant."

PART TWO

the *sexy* art
of *flirtation*

CHAPTER 6

THE EQUITATION OF
FLIRTATION

Men are not so unlike
equines after all.

In horseback-riding-speak, equitation is how you hold your body and your posture when you're riding a horse. The Equitation of Flirtation is how you hold your body and your posture to signal a prospective flirt candidate that you think he's a potential "mount." Even if you've never ridden a horse before, there are lots of parallels between riding and flirting that can help you know exactly what to do in major flirtation situations. By the time you're finished with this chapter, you'll understand that mastering the art of flirting with a man is not so different than mastering a horse—and going for the ride is the best part!

Prior to even the most elementary flirting, it is essential to understand something about the intrinsic nature of your Object of Flirtation, that noble beast known as Man. It's not for nothing that piles of books exist attempting to parse and explain the vast realm of differences between men and women. Likewise, in the world of horseback riding, one of the greatest barriers to riders communicating with their horses is the mistaken idea that horses are anything like people! Men and women have very different personalities. Their minds don't operate the same way. Actions and impulses completely natural to a man are often completely unnatural to a woman. That's why it's so important to get a grasp on the natural instincts of men in order to develop a sympathetic (er, manipulative) understanding of their needs and reactions. So remember, it's a mistake for any woman to believe that male instincts and sensibilities are the same as her own, but by using the pointers from this chapter, you'll be able to adjust for the differences and work your flirting magic.

THE NATURE OF MEN—AND HORSES!

Just like horses, men are rather high-strung (read: nervous) creatures who respond best to quiet and confident handling. Both men and horses have two physical ways of messaging how they feel: the position of their head and the expression in their eyes. Like a horse, a man who is skittish will hold his head up at attention, his eyes will be wide and staring, his nostrils will be distended, and the muscles on his neck will be tight. (Sound like anybody you know?) By contrast, a relaxed, happy man will stand in a casual manner and almost look past you as you approach. Then he will either ignore you or continue eating (or drinking) or give you a welcoming whinny.

If you're moving toward a horse that has been turned out into a paddock, it's critical you make your approach quiet and even. It's not so different from setting your sights on a man who is bellied up to a bar. In both paddock and bar situations, it's reassuring for the animal—human or equine—when you speak calmly and quietly. If it's a horse, your goal out in the paddock is probably to put a bridle and lead on him. If it's a man . . . well, it is much the same. In order to achieve this, you need to start out slowly and move progressively closer until you can easily move in for the kill.

> "Like an unruly horse that isn't being subservient to the desires of its master, you occasionally have to give that horse (read: man) a good hard punch on the nose. That will usually settle who's boss immediately and make for a much better relationship between man (read: that woman) and 'horse.'"
>
> —*Pat*

Confused? Don't be! For example, if your aim is to rest your hand on a man's shoulder, begin by touching him near the elbow. You never walk up to a horse from behind, and the same holds true when approaching a man. Avoid sudden, startling movements or rear approaches unless your intention is to startle him deliberately by grabbing his ass.

The aim here is to take control without the animal realizing that is what you're doing. You want to tame that unruly horse by lulling him into a false sense of security, so he will acquiesce to your every desire.

Dressage, a formal style of riding, is the execution by a trained horse of complex movements in response to barely perceptible signals from its rider. Just like first-rate dressage riders, first-rate flirts have the ability to make what they do look easy. What admiring or envious onlookers seldom realize is the amount of time, hard work, dedication, and experience that goes into top competitive riding—and flirting. Don't be put off if you're new to flirting or because it's been so long since you've competitively flirted that you feel hopelessly out of shape. Remember that just like any ranked horseback rider, even the most skilled and proficient flirt has to begin somewhere, and that she, too, has persevered through her share of disappointments, frustrations, and setbacks.

Horses, as you might know, aren't loved and appreciated for their enormous intelligence. In fact, it's good that they're kind of dumb because given their physical size and strength, nobody would be able to ride them otherwise. Men, of course, are much smarter than horses. And, as a rule, compared to women, they are generally much bigger and stronger. Like horses, men do possess a particular shared trait—both have uncommonly long memories, which makes them capable of holding on to negative impressions and experiences for a very long time. That's why any moment of frustration or anger you reveal to men (and to horses) will cost you many hours of remedial work to re-establish their confidence.

THE MOUNT

In riding and flirting, you need to know how to mount your steed. (Get your mind out of the bedroom, little lady! In this context, "mount" doesn't have anything to do with sex . . . at least not directly. In this chapter, "mount" is a metaphor for seizing control.) Remember your ABCs of Flirting: Approach, Behavior, and Control. When you flirtatiously approach a man and you've made the decision to "ride" him, in essence what you are doing is taking your best shot at managing—if not out-and-out manipulating—the situation. Yes, it is all about control!

In equestrian language, direct mounting is accomplished thus: You stand with your left shoulder to the horse's side and place your hand on top of the horse's neck. Next, you place your left foot in the stirrup, pointing your toe down, and pivot on your right leg to face the horse.

From this position, the next step is to spring up, lift your right leg over the animal's hindquarters, and finally lower yourself gracefully into the saddle seat. In the vernacular of flirtation, direct mounting is accomplished like this: You approach the man, stick out your chest, and spring. It'd be great if you could actually slide your leg over a man's hindquarters, but that's a wrestling move, not flirtation. Metaphorically speaking, once you're "in the saddle," if he doesn't immediately run away from you, you're "in."

The Mounting Block

As with both horses and men, using some kind of mounting block is both useful and safer. A horse-mounting block is any type of small, secure platform that you can use to climb onto the animal. A milk crate or a rock in the field will do in a pinch. A man-mounting block is not usually something physically tangible.

A good example of a mounting block in Flirt World would be an introduction to a guy by a mutual acquaintance. In both horse-mounting blocks and man-mounting blocks, it is crucial that the horse be standing still. You can accomplish this by holding the reins yourself, but it is much easier if you can employ the assistance of another person to hold the reins for you. Why do you want the man to stand still? Because it's so much harder to hit (or hit on) a moving target.

Saddle Up and Take the Reins

Few men, unfortunately, come equipped with reins. If they did, it would be so much simpler to hold on to them! Of course, you can hold on to a man by grabbing him firmly by the lapels, but that usually indicates a high level of intoxication on your part—definitely not recommended! A better way to "hold" on to a man is by asking him to refresh your drink, requesting he watch your seat, or by giving him something personal of yours to keep watch over—maybe your cell phone, for instance.

You might think that this would make a guy feel put out, but actually, the opposite is true. Men love to feel like they are in charge, and they really enjoy coming to a woman's rescue—even if it is just by defending her seat or quenching her thirst. It is all about the "damsel in distress" and the "knight in shining armor" thing. Of course, if he puts your drink down and walks away from it, allows someone else to take your seat, or hands your phone over to someone else to hold while you run to the ladies' room to check your lipstick, immediately abandon him as a Flirt Object and move on to somebody else!

Saddling is a similar matter. Basically you put a saddle and stirrups on a horse as a way to make your ride more comfortable, but also as a way to control him. In horse-riding circles, the saddle, stirrups, blanket, girth, pad, bridle, bit, and sometimes a martingale (a piece of equestrian equipment used as a mild restraining tool) are known as "tack." Outfitting the horse in all this gear is called "tacking up."

You can "tack up" your man by doing any of the following:

⋯⟩ Buy him a drink.
⋯⟩ Involve him in an in-depth conversation in which you employ all of your best flirting wiles.
⋯⟩ Give him your cell phone number or e-mail address.

Getting a Leg Up

In horseback riding, sometimes you need a "leg up" to get into the mounting position. A leg-up mount is necessary when you've tried everything you normally would to get onto the horse but you just can't achieve the mount on your own. What happens here is that someone nearby helps you. The recommended method is for the other person to stand a little behind you and place her hand under your left knee. Customarily on the count of three, that person gives you a boost so you can swing your leg over and up.

In a flirtation leg-up mount, your assistant (i.e., one of your girlfriends) gives you a boost by engaging in some three-party flirting (see Chapter 11 for more details) by calling attention to one of your principal attributes, such as:

----> Your new car
----> Your exciting European vacation
----> Your amazing inheritance
----> The gorgeous empty house with a swimming pool you're housesitting for the weekend
----> Your hot tub

But let the flirter beware here—you could be setting yourself up as a target for a male gigolo, so be sure you choose your attributes wisely!

Good old-fashioned whipped cream is a totally fun thing to eat when you're flirting. It's light. It's delicious. It's also a bit kinky since subliminally it reminds men of . . . semen. Take a long time lapping it up and you'll have any male in the immediate vicinity practically drooling.

Vaulting

Vaulting to a mount directly from the ground is something usually done exclusively by rodeo competitors or Hollywood stunt people. Vaulting is flashy (and useful if you're in a tearing hurry, since it can be done while the horse is in motion), but it definitely requires advanced agility and riding skills. The spring (or vault) must carry the rider right on top of the horse's withers and be powerful enough to allow the rider to straighten her arms. The average equestrian is probably never going to execute this move unless she's out in the field on a fox hunt. Out in the flirt field (which is not so different from a fox hunt), vaulting is still a flashy and nervy move that requires advanced agility, not to mention moxie and chutzpah!

Flirtatious vaulting by definition must be executed quickly and boldly. Use the vault when you want to make an instant strong impression or bid for dominance. The vault isn't suitable for every flirt situation. For one thing, it's brash, which makes it inappropriate in certain situations. (You don't want to look like a glibidiot, do you?) Also, as mentioned earlier, certain men (like horses) may become skittish when you make such a fast move on them. Have fun, but use this mount sparingly.

What happens in a flirt vault is that you take your mount (er, man) by surprise. You say or do something disarming. Some examples of surprising/disarming/flirt vaulting actions include doing the following things within moments of meeting him:

⋯⟩ Asking him if he's single
⋯⟩ Telling him he's the hottest guy in the room
⋯⟩ Planting a big kiss on his lips

Use the vault move very judiciously and only if you're a proven, effective flirt who is certain what the reaction will be.

FINDING YOUR SEAT

Now that you've perfected your mount, it's time to move to the next step. What riders refer to as the "seat" describes how your bottom affixes itself to the saddle, or in bareback riding, the horse's actual back. You hear riders talking a lot about "seats"—who has a good one (never falls off), and who needs to work on hers. In riding, the foundation of a good and effective position rests entirely upon seat. Keep your balance! Don't get anxious and grip the horse with your knees or thighs.

The purpose of developing a good seat in riding is the same as developing a good seat in flirting. It's all about balance, gravity, and keeping you "on." When your seat is off, you are off balance. On horseback, when you're not balanced, your body goes stiff in your efforts to stay on. That stiffness reduces any effectiveness you have through the use of your seat later on. What's worse, any corrections or adjustments you make in an attempt to remedy your seat almost always causes some other body part to stiffen up.

In flirting, as in riding, you want to avoid getting stiff. You want to stay relaxed and balanced. That's the only way you'll be ready to handle whatever the Object of Your Flirtation throws at you, whatever situation, good and bad, that comes your way. In flirting, as in riding, finding your seat takes practice, which is why you have to flirt a lot to get good at it!

Here are some problems and solutions for you to ponder in case you should get thrown off your seat. Hey—it happens to everyone at some point. Just remember, practice makes perfect!

PROBLEM: He says, "Jump in my car—this party's moving to another location!"

SOLUTION: Make sure you know what you want. Are you committed enough to the flirtation to go with him? Don't agree to something that makes you feel uncomfortable.

PROBLEM: He asks, "What movie do you want to see?"

SOLUTION: Be assertive—try to have an answer at the ready. Under no circumstances should you answer, "Whatever you want."

PROBLEM: He invites you to go swimming but shows up with another woman in tow.

SOLUTION: Don't freak! Embrace your inner goddess, cheerily say hi, and then ignore her until you figure out how to use her presence to your own advantage.

Once your flirt seat is secure, the real fun begins! When you are confident about your balance you're free to explore all the basic paces and directions that a good flirtation can take. No matter what the other person does (and just like a horse, a man is apt to wheel, buck, or startle), if your seat is secure, you won't fall off. You'll be secure, you won't go stiff, won't make any wrong moves that could scare him off. Ultimately when your seat is good, you'll be in control, able to ride out the flirt, and hopefully have a great time.

GET YOUR BACK UP

On horseback, your back should be upright, your spine erect, centered directly above the spine of the horse. At the same time, it should be supple enough for the movements of the horse to be absorbed by your hips and the small of your back. It can take years for the human body to adapt to these movements. Your shoulders should be square without being stiff, you must look straight ahead, and above all, you should not look down because to do so can throw you off balance.

The same things hold true when you're in a flirting situation. Your back should be upright, your spine erect. You should be straight but flexible enough to absorb and respond to any surprising movements, motions, or verbiage your flirtation partner flicks your way. Not to mention the fact that keeping your spine erect makes you look taller—and slimmer. And your boobs always look better when you stand up straight!

Work on improving your posture at all times. Remember that old thing called "deportment"? Practice it! Whenever you're walking around town, taking an escalator, sitting at your desk, wasting time at the water cooler with your office mates and friends, be aware of how you're standing. Don't slouch! Besides, every moment of the day is an opportunity for flirtation, especially in an office when hanging around the water cooler. So, sit up, ladies!

YOU'VE GOT LEGS—USE THEM

The legs are the most essential part of horseback riding. It's all about the position of your legs, how the natural V between a woman's legs must shift to accommodate the enormous width of a horse.

When you're riding, you control a horse with your lower legs by keeping them turned in and resting comfortably against the horse's side. Confused yet? Don't be!

On *terra firma*, which is the place where you'll probably be doing most of your flirting, your legs are important because, well, they keep you balanced—but more importantly, *men will be looking at them*. Your legs, in fact, are one of your strongest physical assets when it comes to flirting. Think of them as actual tools you can use to propel and direct your flirt. Use them to get physical! Try these tricks to get your leg on:

⸺⇢ Take advantage of any excuse to get your leg on or at least near that horse, er man. If he offers you a ride on his motor scooter, take it! Wrap your leg close to his. He'll feel it!

⸺⇢ You're in the pool together. Now swim up behind him and lock legs with him.

⸺⇢ You're lying on the beach together sharing a blanket. Briefly drape your leg over his. Make it seem like an accident.

⸺⇢ He's sitting on a bench next to you drinking coffee. Scooch over a millimeter so that your leg brushes up against his.

IT'S ALL IN YOUR HANDS

On a horse, quiet hands are everything. Hands that are flapping all over the place make a horse very nervous and send it mixed messages, which is something all women should think about! Without going into too much detail, in riding, the hands should follow the movement of the horse's head and neck and work as a pair. Contact with the reins should be neither too light nor too heavy, and should be sympathetic to the animal's ultrasensitive mouth. Half of the messages a rider sends to her mount are through her hands

The same is true in female-male relations. How you use your hands is extremely important to a successful flirt! If you gesture a lot when you talk, then your hands are communicating as much about you as your words are. All the more reason to keep them pretty! That means your hands should be clean, your nails well kept (polish is nice but not necessary), your cuticles trimmed. Also be wary of cracked, dry, rough hands. Not surprisingly, dry, cracked hands strike most men as unfeminine. Not to mention, they're unpleasant to the touch. How can you leave him with a soft, memorable caress if you've got alligator skin? Well-moisturized hands speak well of you. So grab a tube of your favorite hand cream and go to town, lady!

Okay, now let's put all of this good hand grooming to use. You can use your hands to get a man's attention. If you can work it, you can use your hands to do the flirting for you:

THE FLIRTY "HI" FINGER WAVE—What's so marvelous about this movement is that it seems so casual and uncommitted. It's also fabulously ambiguous. The flirty finger wave means hello—but it also means goodbye!

THE FACE FRAMER—Cup your hands around your face with fingertips pointed toward your eyes. This helps you draw attention to them, and that's when you hit him with your direct and disarming gaze.

THE LIP GLOSS TRICK—Use your fingertips to touch your lips. This is another way of drawing attention to your mouth. Buy sheer, potted lip gloss, because you have to put it on with your fingers. Men love that!

THE MOISTURE FACTOR—You've heard this once before, but let's reiterate for good measure, shall we? Your hands are one of your most important flirtation tools. Make sure they are attractive at all times. Even if you can't get a real manicure, at least keep your nails nicely filed. Be liberal with your use of hand cream. You want them nice and soft so that when a man happens to touch them, they'll feel nice. Plus when your hands are inviting, men will fantasize about what erotic things you might know how to do with them.

That said, don't use your hands so much that you're mistaken for a marching band conductor.

Here's a quick list of hand Dos and Don'ts:

⟶ DO use your hands occasionally to accent what you are saying.

⟶ DON'T use your hands to underline or boldface every phrase, even if you are highly animated and excitable.

⟶ DO use your hands wisely.

⟶ DON'T point, clap, semaphore, or wave your hands in the air every instant unless you're at a hockey match or football game. Inordinate hand movements create a frenzied atmosphere that almost always makes men shy away from you.

⟶ DO wrap your hands provocatively around the stem of your wineglass.

⟶ DON'T twist your rings around on your fingers or use your hands to pluck at your clothes. Those movements indicate emotional instability or shout that you are extremely bored or anxious, none of which is conducive to good flirting!

⟶ DO use your hands to slowly unbutton one significant button on your sweater or your blouse.

⟶ DO use them to reach out and briefly (!) touch someone.

Just remember that men's eyes will follow a woman's hands. When you're engaged in a flirt operation, never scratch your ears or pick your nose or do anything else gross or nasty. Make your hands work for you—and remember, keep 'em loose. No death grips! Ever!

STICKS AND SPURS

The primary aids in both riding and flirting are the legs, the hands, the seat, and the voice, more or less in that order. But what if you run into trouble and need a little something more?

Aside from these factors, horseback riders also use what are called *artificial aids*. Okay, get your mind out of the gutter! What you have in your bedside drawer is your own business. But the tools you need for your ascension of the spiraling staircase for flirt perfection are right here.

In riding, artificial aids can further help you get your mount to do what you need him to do and to correct him when he steps out of line. These aids include sticks and spurs. While you probably don't want to kick the Object of Your Flirtation with spurs (or maybe you do), there *are* metaphorical sticks and spurs that can be utilized to get you on top and on your way.

As a flirt expert, or future flirt expert, you need to figure out your own arsenal of proverbial sticks to urge your man along and correct disobedience when it arises or occurs. It is essential that you discover some means of correcting early bad behaviors from your Flirt Object before they get out of hand. Once you've got yours, don't hesitate to use them! Every woman has sticks and spurs of her own invention. Following are some troubleshooting tips to make that man behave before he tries to take you for a ride:

> **PROBLEM:** He sort of seems into you, but you get the sense he's checking out the other merchandise.

SOLUTION: Stop eye contact with that man the moment he gets out of line. By withdrawing a little and playing hard to get, you'll get his attention back to where it needs to be—on you.

PROBLEM: He's leaning too close and moving too fast for you.

SOLUTION: Shift your physical position when he starts moving too fast. If necessary, get up and walk away!

PROBLEM: He's become ensconced in a conversation about the '79 series with the bartender while fetching you a drink and you fear you're losing him.

SOLUTION: Use your tone of voice to convey displeasure and get him back into conversation with you.

PROBLEM: Within minutes of meeting you, he grabs your butt and makes a lewd comment.

SOLUTION: Give him a swift kick in the shins. On occasion, a girl might have to do just this to make sure her position is understood and to keep her flirtatious control intact.

A stick isn't just used to reprimand. On a horse, it's often used as a prod. Spurs are great prods too, but most women's shoes unfortunately don't come equipped with them. A favored method for urging a man on in a flirt situation is to laugh. Men respond really well to female laughter. They interpret laughter—with them, not at them—as encouragement. Simply by giggling, tittering, or emitting great gales and peals of laughter at almost anything a man says tells him you are captivated by his company and that you enjoy spending time with him. So laugh, laugh away. It's a woman's secret weapon, make no mistake!

CHAPTER 7

THE ART OF THE TEASE

Telegraph your interest using your *eyes*.
If that doesn't work, just use your fingers and *point*.

Your body speaks a language all its own. Without realizing it, how you sit, what you do with your hands, your legs, even your basic posture reveals volumes about you, namely what you're feeling, what you might be thinking, and, most importantly, if that guy sitting across from you is getting to you.

The thing about body language is you want to be completely in control of it. You want to be aware of what messages you're sending and avoid telegraphing certain information you're not ready to give away. Dumb as they may seem sometimes, men are not exactly knuckleheads when it comes to interpreting a woman's body language. Any reasonably perceptive and intuitive guy you're flirting with is reading many things about you simply by studying your movements.

You can utilize body language to your own advantage by transmitting only the messages you want him to receive, which gives *you* the upper hand. Body language has a lot in common with cell phone text messaging. It's shorthand information, meaning it's quick, direct, and gets right to the point.

BODY LANGUAGE BASICS

Without even thinking about it, women almost always give physical tips that convey their level of interest in a man. The most common body language gestures that reveal at least minimal interest are hair twirling, hair tossing, and leg crossing. When a woman tosses her hair, it comes across as a nervous gesture. What it tells the man is, he's making her a bit nervous. And to his mind, if she's nervous, she must be interested!

On the other hand, hair tossing, like leg crossing, is also a preening gesture. It's a way of calling attention or showing off a gorgeous glossy mane (very sexy) or a terrific pair of gams (ditto, also very sexy!). But there are many other elemental gestures and basic postures that send a strong message to another person, all of which can be used to good effect.

Let's get started describing and interpreting them!

Eye Contact

Usually the first way two people connect is through looking into each other's eyes. Before either of you speaks a single word, the eyes have already telegraphed messages. Messages can range from frank curiosity to cool assessment to shy interest. When you look deeply into a guy's eyes, you're telling him you think he's the most fascinating person in the room. In fact, if you keep your eyes locked on his, what you're saying is that as far as you're concerned, he's the only person in the room!

Full frontal eye contact can be risky, however. It can seem too bold and brazen to those men who are put off by such direct behavior by women. But if you're not the bashful maiden type, frankly gaze. In a way it's a form of natural selection. A guy who is freaked out by your open gaze is probably not a guy for you!

Arm Crossing

When a woman crosses her arms over her chest, it can be interpreted in a number of ways by a guy. It can telegraph the message that she's a vulnerable female creature, an innocent little lamb who feels the need to protect herself from the Big Bad Wolf!

But arm crossing is also a way of telling a guy you don't like him at all and that your fondest wish at the moment is that he'd go away.

Crossing your arms over your chest also is a sneaky way of drawing attention to your breasts. It's a primitive gesture of sexual anticipation laced with sexual anxiety, which a man might correctly read as the woman's acknowledgment of the basic Me Tarzan, You Jane chemistry happening between them.

Leaning Toward Him

The most common form of this is leaning forward when you're sitting across from him. This gesture shows interest and acceptance. In short, it means you just think he's the funniest, cutest, most fascinating creature put on the face of this earth.

But keep your poker face, player-girl! If you go overboard with the lean, you're giving away your whole hand. You want to keep him guessing at least a little bit, right?

If you catch yourself practically falling into his lap, take a deep breath, sit back in your seat, and rest your hands in your lap for a few minutes—at least until you cool off!

If you find yourself leaning away from him, you're either telling him you hate his guts or you're working overtime to not let him know that you're all hot and bothered for him.

Leg Crossing

Leg crossing can be interpreted as a nervous or provocative gesture. Lots of people unconsciously cross and uncross their legs when they're anxious. If you're doing this, the man will correctly intuit that he's some-how "getting" to you. In other words, it's a dead giveaway to the guy that he's unsettled you and his energy has thrown off your equilibrium. On the other hand, if you're deliberately crossing your legs to show off your sexy gams, or deliberately pointing your top leg in his direction, it means you like him a lot. If you can't stop crossing your legs and you're virtually twitching in your seat, again this is an unconscious gesture that clearly tells the man that he's really getting to you. You probably don't want to give him that much power. If he knows you're burning hot for him, he has the upper hand—and you don't want that. If something about him has really got you squirming, get up, take a walk, or go home and take a cold shower!

Hair Twirling

Toying with your hair is a sure sign of nervousness. If you find your-self doing this, take a moment to ask yourself why this guy is making you nervous. Is it because he's too handsome? Too incredibly clever? Is it because you can't get your mind out of the gutter imagining what he would be like in bed? Save your agitation for later—like when you finally fall asleep and have a red-hot dream about him!

Hair twirling can also be a playful gesture. Women with long hair tend to play with their hair. Hair is sexy and twirling and tossing it draws a man's eye to it. But beware: Many guys say it really bugs them when women keep playing with their hair. Talk about sending the wrong message! What some women think is sexy is a major turnoff to some guys.

Lip Licking

This is purely physiological. Forget what they say about "drooling" over a hot guy. When we're aroused and excited, our mouths get dry. If you find yourself licking your lips a lot in the company of a new man, it means that something about him is really getting to you. Watch out!

Lip licking clearly conveys the message that you're interested in a man. It is a very sexy, and overt, type of body language— that is, if it is done correctly. What we are talking about here is a slow, sultry swipe along your lips with the tip of your tongue. Just remember to use this one with caution. Your Flirt Object will probably think you are telling him you want to take him to bed. And maybe you do! If that's the case and you're both equally interested, by all means, lick your lips. It's another way of saying, "Let's go back to your place right now." In other words, it's an action-getter.

It's the little things that count in body language, mostly things you do unconsciously, the stuff you don't even think about. So many gestures are completely nondeliberate. Learn a little about them so you're less inclined to give yourself away.

- **EYE OPENERS:** Dilated pupils reveal your interest. Ditto if his pupils are dilated. There's a good reason to wear dark sunglasses— you won't give yourself away!

- **FOOTSIE, FOOTSIE:** How and where you position your feet is also an indicator of how you feel about someone. A wide stance means you're definitely interested. Feet close together (or knees close together when seated) mean that you're not.

- **LOTSA LAUGHS:** When a woman laughs at just about anything a guy says, it means she's superinterested. The guy doesn't even have to be very funny!

Standing Very Close

When you stand very close to a guy, almost touching but not, it means that you find him irresistible and you want him to know how you feel, or you're deliberately trying to spook him a bit by being very, very subtly aggressive. There are a lot of reasons to get up close but not quite personal. When you're only centimeters away from him, he can smell your perfume, feel the heat of your body, inhale the conditioner you put in your hair. Getting as close to another person as you can be without actually touching him is very, very, hot.

Don't Stand So Close to Me

There are definitely times that you want to put a little space between you and the other person, even if you like him a lot. Sometimes because you like them a lot! That's why you should lean back in your seat when you're across the table from a guy who's really lighting you up. To keep your own balance, you have to literally put some space between the two of you. This is a way to say either, "Hey buddy, slow down," or "I find you awfully hot. I need to back off so I can cool off!"

In the Blink of an Eye

This is an unequivocal indication of nervousness. Is this person unsettling you? Sounds like it. Scientists and forensic psychologists who study body language say that a lot of blinking can indicate that a person is lying. So think about those blinks!

Flared Nostrils

Omigod, this is the mother of all body language signals! Flared nostrils are an irrefutable sign of sexual arousal. If you're talking to a man and his nostrils are flaring, you can bet your booty he's achin' for you. And, um, it works vice versa. If your nostrils are flaring, your nipples are probably hard, too. If you're flirting with a guy and you've both got the nostril thing going, look out. You might have to rent a motel room!

Other Indicators

If you don't want a guy to know that you're jonesin' for him like he's a drug, take a deep breath and take control of your fidgeting, twitching, hair twirling, and jewelry fondling. This kind of stuff is a dead giveaway you're interested. If you don't want the guy to know just how much you want him, knock it off!

Remember, it's important not to show your hand too early in any flirting game. Step back. Focus on something else. Wait for him to make the next flirtatious move, which could be something as simple as him speaking to you. When you feel he's warming to you a bit, you can initiate some subtle physical interaction. You might reach over and brush a spot of lint off his jacket (which is not a bad excuse at all to put your hands on him).

He's So Shy!

What if your flirt quarry is a supershy guy? Openly smiling at a shy guy may be too much for him to handle. In fact, it could scare him right off! Shy guys are hard to read. Their body language often runs contradictory to their true emotions. Shy guys send a lot of mixed messages, and it's up to you to decode them and either flirt them up or move on out. Here are some telltale signs you're dealing with Shy Guy:

···⟩ He looks at you but when he catches you looking back, he avoids eye contact.

RESTAURANT RULES:

10 SMOOTH MOVES FOR

1. Wear totteringly high heels so he's got a reason to take your arm! Neither one of you wants the embarrassment of you tumbling flat on your face. Also, high heels give a girl the butt wiggles, which is very enticing. Shake that booty, please!

2. When you're talking to him, occasionally touch his arm. Your geographic boundary lines are from his fingertips to his elbows.

3. Offer him a bite off your plate. Make sure to offer it to him on your fork!

4. Permit him to order for you. It's an old-fashioned thing to do and therefore chivalrous and sexy. Be sure to mention if you never eat red meat or if you're allergic to shellfish. A date that winds up in the emergency room is a bit of a downer, although many men find women in hospital gowns to be exceedingly vulnerable and sexy (it's the open back thing).

5. Wear slightly dangly earrings with a bit of sparkle that will catch any candlelight. They'll mesmerize him to the degree that he won't be able to take his eyes off you.

GETTING HIM TO EAT OUT
OF YOUR HAND

6. Allow your knee to occasionally bump his under the table. When you make contact, quickly pull your knee away.

7. If you really like him and find him clever and witty, play with your bracelet or fondle your own wrist. Showing your wrist is a sign of submission. On the other hand, if you think he's a time waster, pointedly look at your watch!

8. Train your eyes on his mouth while he's talking to you. Use mental telepathy to communicate to him that you find his mouth very sexy and you're imagining what it would be like to lock lips with him.

9. Wrap your beautifully manicured fingers loosely around the stem of your wineglass. That will make him visualize what your fingers might look like wrapped around his own "stem."

10. When he helps you into your wrap at the end of the evening, lean a bit into him so your bodies lightly connect. If you've generated enough electricity between you, you might get shocked by the spark!

Cardamom, cloves, black pepper, and cinnamon mixed together are considered to be an aphrodisiac. Widely served in trendy coffee bars with hot milk and sugar, chai tea is a well-regarded Eastern Indian stimulant—and a sexy drink to sip while you're flirting him up!

····≥ In group situations, he'll talk to everyone in the room but you, even though he can't take his eyes off of you.

····≥ He'll find an odd way of making physical contact with you—usually through a clumsy or awkward movement.

So what's the right body language to use on Shy Guy? Next time you're schmoozing with him, try one or more of these tips:

····≥ Avoid looking straight into his eyes too much (you'll just make him very nervous).

····≥ When he bumps into you, bump into him right back!

····≥ Touch a shy guy very lightly and in an innocuous place. Steady his hand when he's holding a light for you, or if some part of your bodies brush together, say, "Oh, sorry," in a low and modest voice.

····≥ Ask a shy guy to help you off with your coat or jacket. It'll bring his body close to yours, but in a "safe" and socially correct manner.

COME-HITHER QUIZ

Okay, so now you know a little about body language and how to use it. So let's put your newfound knowledge to the test. Take a look at the following flirting scenarios and see how body language plays a part in the dialogue.

SCENARIO #1

You're in a coffee bar. So far it's your lucky day. You got a table to yourself, you've got your decaf mocha skim milk latte, your biscotti, your newspaper, and your journal at the ready for scribbling down important thoughts. You've just read your daily horoscope ("Innocence and virginity are your themes for the day. You may be questioning your current life situation or the kind of people you are attracting"), when you notice a cute guy looking your way. What do you do?

A.   Look back.

B.   Bury your face in the newspaper.

C.   Spill your coffee on your shirt in surprise that a man is actually looking at you.

D.   Flash a smile.

While both A and D are acceptable choices, D is the truly flirtastic move! No body language says "Let's play!" more directly than a smile.

SCENARIO #2

Let's say something different happens. Say he flashes a smile back, but then drops his eyes down to his own croissant/newspaper/magazine. This means you have to:

A.   Let it go, let it go, let it go—unless a few minutes later you catch him looking at you again!

B.   Quizzically raise one eyebrow. That's like raising a flag, a signal that you're intrigued, and open to him sending more glances your way.

C. Give him a reason to speak to you. The most straightforward yet flirtatious way to do this is to mouth the word, "Hi."

D. If he mouths a "Hi" back, you're in business.

All of these answers are acceptable, depending on your personal flirt style and how aggressive you're feeling that day. Sometimes, you may want to play it cool and other times you just want to go for it!

Scenario #3

Let's say a cute guy approaches your table and sits down across from you. Maybe the place is crowded and there aren't any other seats! He might not say a word. What to do?

A. Pull out your cell phone and put in a call to a friend. Or check your messages.

B. Smile sweetly but let him make the first move. If he doesn't, chalk up the exchange as a pleasant sugar cube that just sweetened up your day. (Most of my favorite flirts never go any further.)

C. Think ahead. If you continue patronizing that coffee bar and that guy continues to put himself in your line of vision and you both do that looking/smiling thing, well, one of these days you're gonna act.

D. Try to start a conversation by dropping him a witty line. Keep it simple. Try something like, "Why do we keep coming here when this coffee sucks so much?" Grin a little when you say it. If he grins back, you're on your way.

If you chose A, go back to the beginning of this book and start all over again! Have you learned nothing? Cell phones are not flirting armor, and should never be used as such.

Answers B and C are a little passive—maybe it's time to revise your 24-Hour Flirt Schedule.

If you chose D, 'atta girl! You're making the most of the situation—something any ace flirter should do.

THAT AWKWARD FIRST DATE—ARRGH!

First dates. Everybody hates them; everybody has to face them. Let's talk about them.

First dates are tricky. For starters, you don't know the guy at all, which obviously makes him almost impossible to read. But before we get into the actual date nitty-gritty, remember the old cliché about first impressions. Here are a few Do Bee, Don't Bee random thoughts about what you should wear:

--➤ Guys love legs, so DO wear a skirt, unless you're doing something outdoorsy, such as hiking, biking, or riding (horseback, that is).

--➤ Even though most first dates are in restaurants, DON'T wear jeans unless it's a barbecue joint. Ditto for most slacks, too.

--➤ DO wear a skirt that hits you right above your knee. Anything really short is way too provocative, but anything really long might remind him of his mom!

--➤ DO wear lipstick, but nothing too red or too shiny.

--➤ DON'T pile on the makeup. The idea is that you want to look great without looking "made up." Whatever you do, go easy on the eye shadow and ditto for the blush.

--➤ If you can't read the menu without them, DO wear your glasses. Squinting is neither sexy nor attractive!

--➤ DON'T fret about glasses making you look studious. Remember that old saw about the sexy librarian?

Okay, let's face it. Every guy is not Prince Charming or even a prince. Some men, even if they are well versed in the art of flirtation, are really just louts. Here are some signs to tell you right away that you're dealing with a flirt jerk:

- He doesn't get up when you come into the restaurant if he's sitting down first.
- He doesn't get the door for you . . . This is a must!
- He lets you pay. You can make a show of pulling out your credit card to split the check, but he absolutely must say, "No, no, I'm getting this," or you should head out!
- He just natters on and on about himself without letting you get a word in edgewise—yuck. It's okay for you to ask him about himself. In fact it's more than okay. It's a terrific flirtation technique to use on guys since every guy in the world just loves to talk about himself. But if he doesn't quit talking about himself to the point where you just wish he'd shut up, find a way to tell him to put a sock in it or just hide for a while in the ladies' room.
- He says something that offends you. If he in any way bores or offends you, decline dessert or coffee and bail!

First-Date Dialogue

What should you talk about on a first date? Well, you can't be flirtatious *all* the time. No matter how quick a wit you are and flirtatiously entertaining, eventually you'll have to have a real conversation or he'll think you're hopelessly superficial and not worthy.

Your checklist for what you should and shouldn't talk about on a first date is as follows:

→ DO avoid discussing previous relationships or why you broke up with your former beau or spouse. The golden rule is "The less said, the better"!

→ DO avoid badmouthing former boyfriends/husbands—even if the guy was a rat.

→ DON'T talk too much about your family, or, even worse, the family you're hoping to have. If you have kids, it's okay to say enough that he knows they're important to you and in your life, but not so much that he gets the impression they're the only thing in your life.

→ DO ask him about his work. Be curious, but not curious like you're a professional investigator or district attorney.

→ DO ask him about his hobbies. If he hasn't got any, he must be a dud!

→ DON'T gripe about your work. Tell amusing anecdotes to illustrate what a dork your boss or office mate is but never say she's a dork.

→ DO mention your interests, what you like to do on your own time. How else will you find out if you've got anything in common other than a hunger to see each other naked?

→ DON'T discuss money. A guy you barely know doesn't need to know the IRS is garnishing your wages or that you can't make your rent. By the same token, don't reveal you've got a trust fund. That's imprudent on a first date.

→ DO be forgiving of little foibles and small accidents. Don't hold it against the dude if he is so nervous being in your totally awesome presence that he knocks over his water glass. After all, you are pretty incredible and he just can't help himself!

His Body Language—What Does It Mean?

So far what we've been talking about is *your* body language. What about his? Guys, just like girls, give themselves away all the time. Once you learn to interpret his body language, you'll have the advantage of knowing what is on his mind. Here are some tips and tricks to help you figure it all out:

→ He pays close attention to every utterance that comes out of your mouth—This means he really likes you and is fantasizing about getting you into bed.

→ He sits bolt upright in his chair—This means he's got a stick up his you-know-what.

FIRST-DATE

FLIRT TIPS

A few handy tips for how to behave on a first face-to-face date:

- When you first approach him, don't kiss him hello. That's way too forward. Just touch or shake his hand.

- Absolutely don't have more than one glass of wine, no matter how tasty it is. Men don't respect women who drink too much and the last thing you want to do is get drunk and sloppy. When the waiter asks you what you want to drink, order your glass of wine or one cocktail but otherwise stick to Perrier or Pellegrino. Make friends with sparkly waters.

- Limit first dates to under three hours. Anything longer is a major mistake.

The only goodbye kiss you should be giving at the end of a first date is that European double kiss thing on the cheeks. No matter how sexy or flirty the evening has been, at evening's end, play it cool. Don't give him any lip on lip action at all. Just make your voice very warm and friendly. That's enough to encourage him!

⋯⟩ He runs to the bathroom every ten minutes—This means he's either got a weak bladder (does the restaurant have a fountain or other water theme?) or he's a coke addict.

⋯⟩ He clenches his hands into fists from time to time—This means he's an angry type of guy or a control freak who isn't getting his way.

⋯⟩ His eyes are rolling up into his head—This means he's about to go comatose or he's bored to death with you.

⋯⟩ He rolls his eyes, period—This means he doesn't believe a word that you say.

⋯⟩ He pats your hand—This means he's patronizing you.

⋯⟩ He rocks back in his chair—This means if you eventually marry him, he'll bust all your good furniture.

First-Date Food

Here's a flirtatiously clever thing to do on a first date. Order something from the menu that you can share together. Sharing food is very sexy, plus it gives you tons of information about the other person, namely is he a pig who just plows through his share so quickly that you feel compelled to eat up, as in eat it or lose it? Or is he an anal compulsive control freak who insists on dividing the thing in half on the plate with a big space between the portions, letting you know right away that he's a guy who likes to set boundaries? Does he offer you the choicest morsels, telling you that he's kind and generous?

While we're talking about flirts in restaurants, do pay attention to his table manners and how he eats his food. Is he a greedy gobbler? Warning! This is a clue that he's going to handle your body in much the same manner. And that's a bummer. You want a guy who takes the time to savor you. . . .

Now that you've mastered these basic elements of flirtatious behavior, it's time to move on to advanced tips!

CHAPTER 8

READ MY HIPS:
ADVANCED TIPS FOR THE FANCY FLIRT IN YOU

A *wink* is as good as a nod to a blind man, although *whispering* in his ear works *faster*.

As you may have noticed, the rudimentary physical language of flirtatiousness doesn't require a huge vocabulary. Winks, nods, smiles, hair fiddling, touching the other person lightly on the arm, a cock of the hip, leaning forward on your elbows when you're seated across from an adorable someone (and incidentally giving them the opportunity to ogle your stunning cleavage, if you're so inclined) are basic physical linguistic techniques. They all relay to the Object of Your Flirtation that he is on your radar and that you're definitely interested. These simple, direct body messages are so clear, they cross all international language barriers. Talk about sign language!

GETTING STARTED— IT'S AS EASY AS SUCKING ON AN ICE CUBE

But if a wink is as good as a nod to a blind man (and yes, that is a line in a Rod Stewart song), for those of you who are ready to advance beyond Flirting 101, there are a plethora of maneuvers to master before you can call yourself a flirt expert. Have some fun experimenting and testing them out, but a word of caution: Don't try them all at once, or on the same guy!

Suck on an Ice Cube

This is a very sexy, very bold, very brazen move. Just remember, it could be, *too* bold and brazen if it's after 11 P.M. and you're still trolling for company, you hussy! You should absolutely, positively make it a policy if you're out on the town and lookin' around to bail by eleven. The decent, respectable people call it a night by then. What's left are the boozers, the bimbos—i.e., the dregs. As my mother used to say, if you don't want fleas, don't lie down with dogs . . . or waste your time flirting with anyone still hangin' at the bar at two in the morning!

When it's the right guy and the right moment, sucking an ice cube can be a very cute, dirty-innocent type of move that most guys just flip for—especially if you team your ice cube sucking with a very "Who me? You think I'm a naughty girl?" expression.

Here's how to do it:

1. Finish your drink. That's key!
2. When you've got your man's attention, slip it in (hey, good double-entendre). Wait a few beats. Don't rush! Take your time and work that ice. Now pick up that ice cube with your fingers; don't just tip back your glass to get the ice into your mouth. Why? Integral to the tease is your fingertips touching the ice. It is even better if your fingernails are painted a sexy shade. Red works, but if you're more of a hot pink girl, go for it!
3. Use your fingers to hold it. Lick it.
4. Now put it back in the glass.

Bet you can't do this three times without having every man within ten yards drooling.

The Head Tilt

This is a great move that allows you to change things up while playing it cool. Rather than coming on like gangbusters loaded up with your best flirtatious lines, try throwing him for a loop by tilting your head and gazing up. This move has an intoxicating effect on men, evoking the image of a fun and mischievous side of a woman. It's the shy, inquiring posture of the head tilt that makes every female seem to be just the slightest bit submissive, an especially appealing persona to cultivate if you happen to be flirting with a particularly aggressive man.

The head tilt is a way of disarming him. It's a very sneaky move that lets you learn a thing or two about him, because it gets him to drop his guard long enough to let you in. And once you're in, baby, find out everything you need to know about this person by posing a gentle flurry of questions and then listening very carefully. Added bonus: The head tilt is a terrific listening posture. It makes you look rapt, even fascinated! This move works best when sitting on a barstool, but you can try it in just about any situation.

Here's how to do it:

1. Cock your head to the left or to the right.
2. Don't be too quick to brush away any hair that slightly falls over your cheek. Let him brush it away!
3. Once you're in position, try out any number of your favorite expressions. Maybe you prefer the gaze of beatific rapture, as in "You are the most fascinating man I have ever met." Or maybe you prefer the amused, slightly skeptical look that says, "You're

so funny and charming even when you don't know your ass from your elbow."

No matter which expression you use, you'll have that man eating out of your hand, or groveling at your feet!

Resting Your Head Against Your Hand

This is a variation on the Head Tilt and works like a charm as a second flirtatious act. The point of this move is to give the impression that you're being held in thrall by whatever the other person is saying and that his words are so meaningful and fascinating that you have to prop up your noggin just to take it all in! In essence, this is an extremely flattering move because it implies that you're totally focused on what the other person is saying. This gesture is disarming and provocative, and it makes men feel important (which is what they love).

Anytime you have your hands near your face you're sending a sexual message. Your hand resting along your cheek or propped under your chin acts as a pointer to draw the other person's gaze completely to your face. They can't help but look right at you, which means they're riveted on your facial expressions.

A few words of warning: If you're going to try this move, whatever you do, don't yawn! Also be sure to be in control of your eyes. If you're bored or exhausted and they're starting to glaze over, he'll see it right away. Instead, if you like the guy and the flirt is going well, use this opportunity to continue sending signals that you think he's totally hot.

Here's how to do it:

1. Perch your chin in the palm of your hand.
2. If you want him to pay special attention to your eyes, position

your hand so that your index finger and middle finger are resting on your upper cheekbone and pointing at your eyes. If you prefer for him to focus on your mouth, try gently tapping your lips with your pinky finger while he is talking.

3. If things are getting hot and heavy and you're liking it that way, slip your pinky into your mouth for a moment. This is an extremely erotic gesture that can appear to the Flirt Object as accidental and spontaneous because you're resting your head in one hand. It won't dawn on him that what you've just signaled is a bit of oral fixation/insertion, because the rest of your body language shows that you're hanging on his every word. In other words, he thinks you're responding to him for his verbal intelligence while in reality you're really tweaking his testosterone!

The Come-Hither Stare

Warning: Proceed with extreme caution! This advanced body language should only be used if you really mean it—it's not for joking or fooling around. If you're not yet ready for advanced flirting, or if you're not sure you're *waaaay* into this guy, then don't use this move, or you could be asking for more than you bargained for.

This openly provocative gesture shows your unquestionable interest right away. Such a direct move has to be handled with care and more than a little degree of caution—be careful of timing and placement of the look that says to a guy, "Get over here—I want you." When a man understands that a woman is giving him the come-hither stare, he can't fail to interpret it as an invitation to sex. This is a high-octane message you're sending with your eyes. It's intense and superhot and lethally potent. When you give a man this look, be prepared for a fast response. He might just jump on you! You want to be careful where you use it. For example, you

EVEN MORE
ADVANCED FLIRT TIPS

Some flirtatious techniques work best if you are what the French call *jeune fille*. Basically, they're nymphet tricks. Use them liberally if you are under thirty—or just feel you are.

1. Toss your hair as much as you can. Toss it until you feel dizzy!
2. Pose, pose, pose. Pretend you are a model and the paparazzi are just lovin' you!
3. Don't just walk. Always turn and pivot. Toss your hair for good measure at the end of the pivot and when you've finished tossing your hair, don't forget to pose!
4. When you're not tossing your hair, flip it!
5. Suck in your tummy and stick out your chest. Do this even when you're waiting in line for the bathroom. You never know who might be on the way out of the men's room!
6. When you're in a club and watching the band, mouth the lyrics to all the songs. Better yet, if it's a really noisy club, sing the words out loud.
7. Wear very high heels. Mince, don't walk.
8. Whether you're actually dating or only flirting with certain members of the band, keep bringing water bottles to the edge of the stage. Act like a "band girlfriend" even if you're not!
9. If your high heels are stilettos, hop in them like a bunny. Use your imagination to pretend you've got a pom-pom on your ass. That'll help remind you to shake it, baby, when you're not posing it.

wouldn't want to pull a stunt like this late at night on the subway.

Of course, there are stares and there are *stares*. If your stare lasts only a few seconds and then you break away, that can be the first step in getting a man you find attractive to look at you. If he stares back, and the next eye contact that happens is you catch and hold each other's gaze, he may come to you from across the room (this is a good move to practice at a crowded party). This gives you an opportunity to begin talking/flirting face to face.

You can also use the come-hither stare on a person you are already dating (even married to or living with). In this case, you are telling him that it's time to leave the party because you're so hot for him that you have to get him alone!

Here's how to do it:

1. Fix your gaze on the Object of Your Flirtation, penetrating him with your stare.
2. Use mental telepathy to transmit the message, "You're hot, you're hot, you're hot."
3. If you are feeling bold at this point, let go of his eyes and run your own gaze like a flashlight up and down the length of his entire body.
4. If you're really brazen (this is best if you already have some carnal knowledge of that person), hold your stare on his fly . . . smile . . . and then drag your eyes back to his eyes. This gets a man every time! Be sure you're really into him before you try this move, though—or you could be playing with fire!

The Sideways Glance

The sideways glance works best when you're trying to catch the attention of someone seated or standing to the right or left of you. It's a glance best executed quickly—after all, it's a glance, not a stare! This move conveys to another person that you've taken notice of him and that you are inviting him to notice you!

Sideways glances are great to do in public places where you find yourself seated on a bench. Those viewing benches in art galleries are good, as are park benches, banquette seating, and so on. It also works well in very close quarters, like when a cute guy is seated next to you on a plane.

The nature of the sideways glance is covert—think of it as a stealth action. It usually takes a few sideways glances before the other person even notices that you're looking. Start out by looking anywhere but at that person's face. You could begin by directing your sideways glance to something that person is reading. Your first sideways glance might be directed toward the newspaper in his hand, and then you can move on to a glance at his hand. Your sideways glances can come fast and furious—lots of abbreviated looks that let you cumulatively take in that person's attire (nice shoes, an outstanding tie, perfectly chewed-up leather jacket), interests (reading material, laptop he is working on), physical appearance (thick hair, sexy throat)—all of which add up to give you:

A. Something you might use as a way in, something to comment on, and
B. Time for *him* to sneak in his share of sideways glances back at *you!*

There are two ways to deliver the sideways glance.

Sideways Glance #1

This one gives the impression that the other person is largely invisible and that you're noticing them the way you might notice a shadow or a dog that just happened to cross your periphery.

1. Cast your glance out of the side of one eye, making the glance only a little more than a flicker.
2. Repeat this flicker until the guy looks back. You might have to repeat this three or four times before that person returns your glance. Some guys are so self-absorbed that it takes a long time for them to get your message.

If you have to do it more than five times, just move on. Lack of response either means he's noticed your glancing and is rebuffing you, or he's too engrossed in whatever he's doing to notice. It's true that with some men, you need to whack them over the head to get them to notice you—but do you really want to be that bothered? Move on and don't take it personally when a guy doesn't notice you. It's his failure. You've got a bright flirting future ahead of you.

Chocolate at one time was banned from monasteries because of its sexy reputation. It's filled with lots of stimulants to make you even more flirtastic. Chocolate contains caffeine, phenylethylamine, which is in the amphetamine family, and theobromine, another mild stimulant. Maybe it's the combination of these three natural ingredients that gives chocolate its reputation for giving eaters a "lift." It is known that eating chocolate lowers inhibitions, and if lowered inhibitions make you a better flirt, eat away!

1. Focus all your attention on the other person out of the corner of one eye, but hold the glance for several beats, six or seven seconds is good.
2. If necessary, count off the seconds to yourself—silently! This is a very purposeful eyeball game. It should be delivered with a perfectly deadpan face.

The message you want to convey is, "I'm looking at you, but I'm not entirely sure if I like what I see." If your glance-ee wants to play, he will most certainly return your glance with his own.

Important tip: This move is best done when wearing a lot of sexy eye makeup. Mascara is a must! The most intense thing you can do here is to devour your man with your eyes in public. That's practically an obscene act!

Sticking Out Your Tongue

As an adult woman, sticking out your tongue is a lighthearted move, usually interpreted as playful, but at the same time it's wickedly provocative, like wearing a schoolgirl outfit when you're anything but! Sticking out your tongue is also provocative in the truest sense of the word because it's meant to provoke. It's an invitation, the kind of gesture that says you're game for flirting and oh so ready to play. It's also a mild fighting gesture, a sort of "put up your dukes and let's rumble" move that tells any man you stick out your tongue to that you're not above a good spar.

Here's how to do it:

1. Channel your inner kid and initiate the exact same expression you had on your face when you were in elementary school and

you stuck out your tongue at a boy that you liked/hated.

2. To pull off this flirt, your eyes should be smiling even as your stuck-out tongue is saying "Nyah, nyah" or even "Eff you!"

If you've got a gamine face, a pixie haircut, or are adorably freckled and can get away with pigtails, this is an especially cool move.

Sighing

A common misconception is that sighing is a turnoff. The truth is, if you know how to work it, it's fiendishly flirtatious because it is such a subversive move. For one thing, sighing calls a great deal of attention to the person sighing, especially if the sigh falls into the category of a major exhalation—an emotive sound that practically screams, "I'm so bored. Rescue me!" Sighing is an incredibly suggestive gesture that has been practiced for centuries by women who know precisely how sexy they look when they are pouting.

The effects of a good sigh and what message it sends to a man can be more effective than any other technique. Sighing is a primitive mode of communication, but it's a great tool. When was the last time you sighed to yourself? It's a sound meant to express an emotion to another person—boredom, annoyance, exasperation, and, on occasion, sadness.

OKAY, BRACE YOURSELF: A lot of guys are turned on by sad ladies. These are the men who love putting themselves in the role of rescuer or knight in shining armor. Nothing gets their juices flowing faster than a damsel in distress. There are men who will correctly interpret sighing as a sign for them to jump in and fix whatever is wrong that's making that woman unhappy. Sighing also presents a natural opportunity for a man to say to a woman, "What's wrong?" And while this isn't exactly a flirt line, it is a wonderful opener. Guys Who Love Making Things Right are suckers for Girls Who Sigh.

How do you do it? Take a gander:

1. Take a deep breath and then theatrically exhale. You can do this two different ways: Emit a small sound, indicating just the teensiest tinge of displeasure or regret; or you can go the major and dramatic route, and let out a gale of a puff. This has the added benefit of really drawing attention to your breath-raised breasts.

2. For additional effect, cross your arms over your chest. Contrary to popular belief, folding your arms over your chest doesn't always indicate that you are closed off and unapproachable. This posture can also suggest great vulnerability. Plus, crossing your arms over your chest also draws attention to your breasts simply because you're trying to cover them up!

3. Now, lean back a bit in your chair and look off into the distance with sad, puppy-dog eyes.

The Chin Thrust

Chin thrusting is an assertive flirting gesture. Basically you are using your chin as a pointer, a way of saying, "Hey, you, over there! I'm lookin' at ya, so pay attention!" This move requires a strong jaw, and it's a move best pulled off by a strong woman. If you fit the bill, use it!

You might want to practice this in a mirror before taking your show out on the road. Here's how to do it:

1. Focus your gaze on the person you wish to flirt with. As soon as you make eye contact, boldly thrust your chin in his direction.

FLIRTATIOUS WAYS TO SAY

"I'M DIGGIN' YOU"

Try some of these coy tips and tricks to tell a guy you think he's pretty groovy—and to put him in a "let's get it on" mood:

- Ask him to kiss you in an unusual location. Like the back of your knees. Unusual physical locations are fun, too, like in the kitchen, in an elevator, just about anyplace other than a bedroom.
- Tell a guy you love it when a man reads aloud to you. Just make sure he's not reading the penis-biting scene from the novel, *The World According to Garp*. Ouch.
- Instant messaging your boyfriend with sexy messages is cute. Take it a bit further by sending him a coy text message on his cell.
- Offer your flirt object a head to toe massage. Don't scrimp on the warmed almond oil. If you're very bold, suggest taking a bath together.
- A penetrating look can indicate you're looking straight into someone's soul.
- When you're out with a group of people, talk to other guys. This will trigger feelings of jealousy and possessiveness, which will undoubtedly pay off later when your guy wants to show you once and for all that he wants you all to himself.
- Shop together. It doesn't have to be anything special. Shopping for new floor mats for your car can be a flirtatious experience!
- Using your eyes only, flirt with someone you've never met in a location that you don't ordinarily associate with flirting—like while you're doing a daytime chore or when you're at some event like your little brother's high school graduation that is being held in some overheated, overcrowded gymnasium. Your mission is to make eye contact with someone, and it is even better if that someone is clear across the room. The whole flirt shouldn't last for more than a few seconds. The only requirement is that you use only your eyes to make him look back.

Make sure your gaze is steady and open and direct.

2. When the Object of Your Flirt opens his eyes wide in surprise (and trust me, this is the usual response), follow up with another physical gesture, which can either be the universal finger wave for "come here," or use your head again as a pointer to tell the other person where you want him to be.

Suck In Your Stomach

Sucking in your stomach is a very sexy gesture. This is a fairly classic move, but if you've never tried it before, you should work it into your flirting repertoire the next time you're out and about.

Sucking in your stomach improves your posture (it's nearly impossible to suck in your stomach unless you are sitting or standing up straight), causes you to shift your pelvis, and shows off your body. It's a great covert flirt move, so no one will really notice if and when you're doing it.

It also draws men's eyes to your middle area, which according to the ancient text of love, the *Kama Sutra*, is the core of your sexual universe. Sucking in your stomach also makes you feel sexy. Try this move when you're wearing something midriff baring, like low-slung jeans or a bathing suit.

Here's how to do it:

1. Stand up straight. Inhale. Hold in your stomach.
2. Try to keep your tummy tucked in at all times, even when you exhale.

By the way, this is a great isometric exercise for strengthening the abdominals, which means that you're multitasking. You're getting in some physical exercise and flirting all at the same time!

Sticking Out Your Chest

Sticking out your chest is such an obvious gesture that many women forget it is a primo advanced body language flirt. You don't have to have big boobs or be sporting cleavage to make this move work, either. Small breasts are as sexy thrust out as big ones. It is equally effective in a form-fitting turtleneck sweater or snug T-shirt.

Sticking out your chest is a primitive way of saying to a man, "I'm a woman. Check me out." Of course if you exercise good posture and never slouch, your chest will always be stuck out—which, of course, is not a bad thing.

Here's how to do it:

1. Stand or sit up straight.
2. Roll back your shoulders while at the same time keeping them relaxed. (Avoid walking around with your shoulders high in the air. That's a tense look and definitely not flirtatious!)
3. Act as though you are relaxed and extremely confident.

The key to this posture is to exude self-confidence. And exuding self-confidence is very sexy—in fact, it's the ultimate aphrodisiac.

OTHER ADVANCED TECHNIQUES

Below the waist is one of the most important areas for body language. When a woman speaks to a man using the anatomy below her waist, she's really talking.

Your behind—that is your hips, your posterior, and the backs of your upper thighs—is in many men's Most Erotic Erogenous Zones when they're checking out women. Pay close attention to how you use your backside. It's major!

Let Your Rump Do the Talking

In the greater vernacular of body linguistics, having a great behind is . . . priceless! Unfortunately most women are sadly insecure about their butts. We always think they're too big, too wide, too soft, too low, too round, too dimply, too jiggly—just too, too! But before you dis your der-riere, you should know that a big, high behind sends a powerfully sexy message. It's a subliminal siren call to booty men everywhere. So first thing you need to do above all else is start lovin' your bottom. Because for every woman out there who hates her behind, there's a man out there who would give the world to worship it.

That said, letting your butt do the talkin' is a time-honored female to male communication. That's why you should have a repertoire of booty tips ready to work for you at all times, including:

> ⋯⋯⟩ TWITCH YOUR HIPS—Twitching your hips is just like winking. It's fast. It's flirty. It indicates interest. Twitching is like flicking. Horses twitch their behinds all the time. For human gals to get the motion right, imagine there's a fly on your behind and you want to do just one single move to get it off—but not using your hand. Don't overuse the twitch. It should also be done quickly—just like winking.

> ⋯⋯⟩ SWIVEL YOUR HIPS—To execute a neat hip swivel, cock one hip.

> ⋯⋯⟩ PERCH YOUR BUTT—That's right, perch your sweet cheeks up on a ledge, such as the corner of a table. Very sexy. Warning: This requires good balance!

→ SHAKE YOUR BOOTY—Some girls have really got this one down, although it does take nerve. Channel some Carmen Electra energy if you don't have the natural genetics for this move

→ JUST STICK IT OUT—Be proud of your posterior, no matter its size. Trust me, there are plenty of guys out there who are crazy for your butt, even if you aren't. So stop trying to hide it when you could be showing it off.

All these moves tell a guy that he's dealing with a real woman and that if he knows what's good for him, he better not mess up. More than any other body part, a woman's behind and how she uses it are the essence of her femininity and her intrinsic erotic power. Every man notices every woman's butt. Since they're so aware of it, you should be aware of it, too!

How should you use your butt? Very consciously. Know that male eyes are on it even in the most mundane situations, like when you're unloading your grocery cart at the A&P. It's up to you to decide whether you feel like showing it off, or if you'd rather pull your sweater down over it to hide it from sight. Just *never* forget you've got it, because no man in your presence does!

Keeping a Leg on It

Legs are inherently very sexual. They're what you wrap around the other person during hot moments.

Here are some ways you can flirt with your legs:

→ CROSS THEM—Leg crossing distracts a man's attention. It makes him look at you. It creates a kind of commotion that goes straight to the sex part of a guy's brain.

---> OPEN THEM—Your legs are columns leading to your most mysterious spot. When you open your legs it's a way of saying, "The door's open. I'm letting you peek in."

---> CLOSE THEM—Again, legs are a conduit to the crotch. When you close them you're telling the man you're closing the door to that particular entryway. Think of your legs as the gateway to your queendom. You can't fail to grab a guy's attention if you use them smartly.

---> BARE 'EM IN A BRIEF SKIRT—Repeat after me: Men love skirts. Pants may make more sense for your lifestyle, but just remember, guys love skirts. (Skirts that have a slit up the side are especially sexy.)

---> PRESS THEM—Press your legs against someone for a moment and then take the contact away. This is a major tease because it seems so accidental, as in, "Did she or didn't she actually touch me?"

---> PLAY KNEESIES—You know by now that footsies is an essential flirt move, but you can also play a game of kneesies to heat things up. It's a fun thing to do under the table! You could also wrap your lower leg around the other person's lower leg. This is a powerful sexual message that unequivocally says "I want you." But if you're going to use that move, be prepared to make good on that promise.

Stuff Your Panties in His Pocket

Okay, so this is pretty outrageous, and it's obviously not a move you want to use if you're going for a Girl Next Door kind of flirt. Don't even think about trying this move unless you're supremely confident, a super vixen, ready to get it on, and have outstanding underwear. Cramming your panties in a man's pocket is tantamount to scrawling "I want you and I want you right now" on your forehead. This move is not a teasing type of flirtation. It's a clear-cut invitation to sex.

Here's how to do it:

1. Go into the ladies' room.
2. Wriggle out of your underwear.
3. Approach the man with whom you've just been flirting your buns off and sidle up beside him.
4. Discreetly slip the panties, which you have secretly balled up in your hand, into his trouser pocket.
5. Don't say a word when he asks, "What was that?"
6. When he puts his hand into his pocket and encounters your silky, soft lingerie, lock your eyes on to his.
7. Keep your expression neutral except for the most subtle of smiles.

If everything goes as planned, you'll soon be in his arms. If not . . . well, he probably thinks you're awfully forward and he won't be asking for your phone number anytime soon.

CHAPTER 9

FROM FLING TO THING—
HOT MOVES TO KEEP YOUR NEW GUY INTERESTED

In every *flirtatious* relationship,
there is a *follower*
and there is a *leader.*

Your initial flirtatious ways helped you get the guy of your dreams, so how do you keep things hot now that you've gone from "fling" to "thing"? This chapter will help you take hold of the reins and keep the flirtation alive in any situation!

Flirting has a lot in common with partnered dancing, like the tango. There are basically two kinds of flirts. There are flirters (leaders) and the flirtees (followers). And unlike dancing, the flirter does not always have

to be the man! While the flirter is the one who prompts or initiates activity, it does take two to tango.

The flirtee is the recipient, the one being flirted *with*. The flirtee often is perceived to be the subordinate or secondary position. The flirtee is the one laughing at the jokes, not telling them. It's a mistake to underestimate the power of the flirtee position, however. Don't ever think of it as passive.

It's imperative that the flirtee be able to hold up her end of the conversation.

She must be able to respond and react to whatever the flirter throws out. At times, she also has to be ready to take the lead by drawing the flirtation in another direction or to a different level. In every good flirt, there is a good deal of repartee. It is not unusual or undesirable in the course of a flirt for the roles to flip—for the flirter to become the flirtee, and vice versa. If there is a habitual position you always take in your flirtations, try changing it once in a while. In fact, change it the next opportunity that comes up where you can flirt, or go out with your girlfriends on a commando mission or small flirt detail.

HOW TO FLIRT LIKE A PROFESSIONAL

In their day, courtesans were Flirtation Experts. The word *courtesan* is derived from the male-oriented term *courtier*, which means "an attendant of the court."

During the Italian Renaissance, certain beautiful and talented women became the companions of princes, bankers, or any male of significance and importance. Far from mere eye candy or window-dressing, these witty, educated, charming, and highly sophisticated ladies had an important role in society where they wielded their power and influence. Traditionally courtesans assumed the role of being beautiful arbiters of sexual intelligence.

Courtesans also excelled in the arts of how to entertain and please a man. They completely understood the seductive and entrancing powers of dancing for a man, bathing him, rubbing him, and massaging his feet. They were expert physical flirts. Of course, a courtesan's role went far beyond merely flirting. Above all else, her job was to please a man sexually. Still, that doesn't mean we can't learn a thing or two from these experts. As a modern-day flirt, you can borrow these techniques and put a contemporary spin on them to bolster and empower your own flirtations with your favorite guy—and this chapter will show you how.

This whole thing may sound very old-fashioned, but be assured that courtesans had plenty of power. In many ways courtesans led a completely enviable lifestyle, using their brains and their bodies to enjoy all the benefits of marriage (property, financial stability, and companionship) without any of the annoying social constraints. In the company of their adoring and often worshipful patrons, courtesans were the ones who got to go out at night and live it up, while the legitimate wives of these gentlemen were forced to stay at home, sequestered away almost like prisoners in their own homes. Yuck to that!

Historians of the courtesan culture believe the first courtesans started in classical Greece. They thrived during the Italian Renaissance and in eighteenth-century Japan (where they were called *geisha*), although the term *courtesan* most accurately refers specifically to those women of the European Renaissance. These women were masters of disguise and sexual intrigue. Sometimes they would dress like virgins or widows to fool government officials who wanted to tax them, while at other times they would showily venture out wearing 10" heels. It was not uncommon for a courtesan to go out for a night on the town in the company of a group of smitten men. These women were early supporters of cosmetics since they often dyed their hair and always wore makeup, even on their breasts. Courtesans also had a huge influence on fashion. Among all women, they were always the best dressed!

Courtesans were also serious game players, skilled at everything from intricate card games to fanciful boudoir activities. A favorite bedroom game in Venice was to act out the story of Leda and the Swan.

So now that you know a little bit about your flirtatious predecessors, it's time to put that knowledge to use in the modern day and make your own history.

DANCE THE NIGHT AWAY

Dancing has a long and erotic tradition. Think of the custom of dancing girls, like in the great days of the Turkish Empire when in the city of Constantinople harem chicks did their thing wearing face scarves and gauzy trousers. The Romans enjoyed their own version of dancing girls. Do I hear the word "orgy"? Long before that, in the realm of legend and mythology, there lived a beautiful young woman called Scheherazade. She danced and told thrilling stories to captivate and subdue a mean and miserable king, not simply to amuse him, but to save her own ass. As the legend goes, the king had been turned into a cuckold when his first wife cheated on him. He had her beheaded by way of punishment. For years afterward, every night he requested that a beautiful young virgin be sent to him from the countryside. After he "married" her and had his pleasure, he would have the woman killed so he would never have to endure being cuckolded by a cheating wife again. Determined to break the chain of murders and to stay alive, Scheherazade adroitly avoided having sex with him, instead pleasuring him with her dancing and stories—in other words, *flirting* with him. She made herself so indispensably entertaining that over a period of 1,001 nights he fell in love with her and made her his true queen!

Modern dancing girls know their way around a dance floor. Some spend their whole lives practicing in front of the mirror in their bedroom, while others were just born with the moves. You don't have to take a slew of lessons at Fred Astaire (although if you've got two left feet, it helps) or have years of jazz, tap, or ballet behind you to produce smooth moves.

Flirtastic Dance Moves

If you love to dance, and you love to flirt, then combining these two moves should be a simple, easy way to have lots of fun. The best way to begin flirting with a man on the dance floor is to ask him to dance. Why wait around for him to ask you when you can take matters into your own hands? Asking him to dance shows leadership and makes you the flirter and him the flirtee, no matter who is leading! Once you've got him on the dance floor, you can downshift gears and let him take the lead, settling into your flirtee role.

Once you're in his arms, you can gradually reveal your charms. Smile. Look into his eyes. Rest your fingertips lightly but firmly on his shoulder. Your hands are touching. Your hips are synchronized. Now's the time to put your best flirtee powers to use:

⸺> Whisper something into his ear. It doesn't matter what you say as long as you keep your voice low and quiet. "Umm, this is nice," works very well. Whatever you say to a man when you're dancing it is sort of like pillow talk. What matters is the physical proximity.

⸺> Breathe softly next to his ear. Your warm exhalation into that sensitive body part will send a current of electricity coursing through his body like a pleasant shock.

⸺> Allow yourself to melt into his body. You're very close. He can smell your perfume, your shampoo, your body heat. Take advantage of the dancing to get in even closer to let him really inhale you.

⸺> Pretend to stumble. If he thinks you're going to fall, he's going to catch you. Now you've got a reason to really grab on to him!

⸺> Look into his eyes. At some point in your dancing, take advantage of the fact that your faces are right next to each other. This is intimacy! Very hot!

NOTE:

When you're flirting on the dance floor, make sure the Object of Your Flirtation sees you dancing with another man, if only for a few minutes. This is an excellent use of the third-party flirt (see Chapter 11). Seeing you move with other men is a turn-on. It brings out the primal male sense of rivalry! Also you're letting him appreciate how sexy you look on the dance floor. While you're at it, make sure to periodically focus your gaze specifically on him.

Slow Dancing

Slow dancing is really hot. You're holding each other close. You're gazing into each other's eyes. If you think about it, there's not much two people can do together that's as sexy or as intimate. Remember *Dirty Dancing*? Fast or slow, hot and heavy, or sweet and simple, it was all about the intimacy of two people finding a rhythm together. This is a chance to really get to know your guy—you're in his space and he's in yours. Don't be caught off guard by your discovery that he's really turned on by you. The famous Mae West line, "Is that a pistol in your pocket or are you just glad to see me?" comes to mind here!

If you want to get in even closer to him, put your head on his shoulder or right up against his neck. Instant skin contact. You'll know how he feels about you by the rapid thump of his heartbeat.

Fast Dancing

You're out dancing at your favorite club. You're really working up a sweat. Your man is keeping right up with you—that's why you chose him—because he can keep up with your beat! How can you get closer but not stop dancing? Try grabbing his hand and using it to execute a cool move, maybe a touch of jitterbug? Or just get really close to him and dance in his space. Try turning your body away from him. Dance so he can stare at your backside.

Dancing with Another Woman to Get His Attention.

Using another woman as a foil is a great way to flirt while you're dancing. Do your sexiest dancing with her and have fun with it. Most guys have a heavy girl-on-girl fantasy reel they like to play in their heads, so use that basic male fantasy to your best advantage and work it, girl!

Barefoot Contessa

Bring out the foot fetishism in your guy by dancing for him barefoot. It might not be the best choice if you're out on the dance floor, but dancing in your bare feet can be even sexier than dancing in high heels. Whether you're on a moonlit beach or in your very own living room, it's a flirty and romantic thing to do. It's also a great chance to show off your perfectly formed arch and your pretty pedi!

Dance in the Rain

Having a dance in the rain can be a very sexy thing. The next time you and your boyfriend are caught in a downpour, pull him close for a little dance. Don't worry about your hair, silly! Dancing in the rain is the move of a joyous spirit, a spontaneous woman who finds sensual pleasure from every natural situation. Men respond to that. And if your shirt gets so wet it looks like it has been pasted to your body . . . that's hot.

Dance in Your Underwear

Obviously you're not going to do this unless you know your Flirt Object very well. This move is fun because it's really intimate, but it's really playful and a great way to show off what you've got. Plus now that

MARRIED—WITH FLIRTING

Married people definitely should flirt. One of the secrets of the happiest marriages is that the partners never give up on flirting or playing flirt games. Here are a few ideas to keep that sense of play going in your married life:

- Try a fun pick-up line. Walk straight up to your partner (especially in front of other people you don't know very well) and say, "Do I know you?" The more deadpan the delivery, the better!

- Be someone else for an evening—it's a fun way to spice things up. Try wearing a wig. It's surprising how easy it is to adopt a different persona! Discover for yourself if it's true that blondes have more fun.

- Play footsies under the table. This isn't just for the resident singletons of the world! Let your hubby know you're hot for him with a little flirty foot play. See how worked up you can make the other person without letting anyone in your proximity be the wiser.

- Create a special signal between the two of you when you're out that keeps you in close contact even when you're chatting with someone else. It could be a simple look or perhaps a code word. Or it could be a private text message you send from your cell phone.

- Pass funny notes. This is an especially flirtatious and amusing thing to do if you're stuck for a weekend at your mother-in-law's.

- IM (instant message) each other throughout the day. Hint at delights and surprises to come when you finally do get together.

- Make up a new language that only the two of you understand. Pig Latin works. Channel that old TV show *Mork and Mindy*. "Nanoo, nanoo." (You might have to Google that to find out what this means.)

- Go on a shopping spree together. Stick to high-end stores, luxury merchandise. Pretend he's your sugar daddy and you're his little babe. You don't have to buy anything, but do try anything and everything on!

you're stocked up on outstanding underwear (see Chapter 3), it's time to show it off. Definitely dance for your man in it. What's sexier than giving your guy a private dance show? Hint: This move is not recommended for clubs, parties, or other social events—that wouldn't be flirty; it would be frightening!

Dance Your Head Off

It's really erotic when a woman seems to get so carried away by her own dancing that she is totally focused. You don't have to dance wildly to dance your head off. What it takes is to get into the groove. Really listen to the music and absorb the rhythm. When a man watches a woman dance this way it's a very potent thing. What it does is push the man into imagining what this woman is like when she's in the sex groove, when someone is making love to her or she's pleasuring herself. This is hot stuff.

MASSAGE

Rubbing your way into someone's orbit is a tried and true flirtatious technique. Besides, it's an excellent excuse to reach out and touch someone—someone you find attractive! Touch, you probably know, is one of the most potent senses. It's incredibly intimate to make contact with another person's flesh. All you need is a bottle of lotion and imaginative hands, and even a few moments of massage can leave an indelible imprint.

Here's the rub: Your attitude is everything when giving a guy a massage. Say you really like the guy a lot but, as of yet, nothing seriously intimate has happened between you. Offering to give him a little rub can definitely jump-start further intimacy! But it also lets the guy know that you find something about him touchable. Desirable. That you're interested in more physical contact.

If you're just getting to know a guy, and you don't want him to know that you find him hot and sexy, keep your cool and channel a professional massage therapist during the massage. By keeping it professional, you will mask, or at least temper, your desire so the guy won't realize right away you're practically creaming for him.

If you've already been really intimate and your hands have explored much or all of his body, use it to your advantage. If he groaned with pleasure when you were running your hands down his sides, do it again. And again. And again!

Neck and Shoulder Massage

The back of the neck is one of the most erogenous zones of the body. It holds a gazillion supersensitive nerve endings. Along with the shoulders, it's the place most men hold their tension. Any man will appreciate the offer of a neck and shoulder rub. Don't be afraid to knead deeply. Only quit applying pressure if he says "Ouch." Otherwise, squeeze those broad shoulders and really work the back of his neck. At the end when he's totally relaxed, try this final trick to really turn him on: Run one finger up the back of his neck swiftly in a light, nearly tickling way.

Back Massage

The back is a great place for a rub, and it's a great excuse to get your guy to take off his shirt and lay down in front of you. This situation can be very flirty because you're in control—you've got him in a prone position. His face is hidden. You've got your hands on his bare back. What to do with him is up to you. Oh, the possibilities!

For an extra sexy touch, you can straddle him as you massage him. Begin the actual massage by rubbing his shoulders and then try long strokes down the middle of his back. Alternate short strokes with long ones and ask for plenty of feedback regarding how much pressure. When you get all the way down to the base of his spine, rub your thumbs firmly and evenly just above his butt cheeks. This is a sure turn-on move, and it's oh-so-sexy.

Head Massage

This may sound a little goofy, but it's actually very intimate. Think about how great it feels to get a shampoo when you're at the salon! When your hands make contact with his scalp, you're sending electric currents coursing through him. This is powerful stuff.

This simple move will give your guy a little taste of heaven, and score you extra points in the Flirtation Expert department.

Begin by kneading his temples and work your way around to the back of his neck. When you feel him relaxing, move up to the top and the back of his head. Use your thumbs and your index and middle finger to work circles all over his head. Don't be surprised when his eyes shut and he falls into a state of babylike bliss.

Foot Massage

If you want to wow a guy, offer to give him a foot rub. The feet are filled with nerve endings and once he gets past the ticklish part, this is a great way to relax him *and* turn him on at the same time. According to practitioners of Chinese medicine, the balls of the feet are very sensitive and very powerful, so be sure to pay plenty of attention to the balls of his feet and his toes. Word of warning: Before attempting a foot rub, make sure you ask your guy to wash his feet!

Here's what to do once you've gotten his shoes off:

1. Begin by rubbing the ball of his foot. Rub it with your thumbs in a circular motion. Occasionally just bear down hard.
2. Place your fingertips on either side of his ankle bone and rub in a downward motion. Squeeze his heel.
3. Take each toe and individually massage it. Begin with the big toe and work your way down to the pinky toe.
4. Take his foot in both your hands and press your two thumbs into the area just below the ball. Don't press too hard. At this point his foot should be totally relaxed and warm in your hands. If it's not, start over.

HAIR PLAY

While hair brushing and shampooing has its place in erotica in times past, not nearly enough attention has been paid in modern times to men's fascination with feminine hair. There's a direct correlation between male sexual desire and female hair. It must be hard-wired into the male animal that female hair is alluring, one of the things about a woman that makes her attractive to a man. Hair is one of those primitive sex signals deeply programmed and embedded in our DNA. That's why you should always make sure yours is touchable and appealing. Nothing turns off a man faster than a woman who screams, "Don't mess up my hair!"

Hair play can work for you or for him. If you happen to have a head of long, sumptuous hair, invite your man to brush it. The idea is for him to pleasure *you* with slow, rhythmic strokes. If he's doing his job properly, you'll be cross-eyed with pleasure and he'll be suffused with awesome power because he's in control. Or you could brush his hair (assuming he's got hair), which will make him the one cross-eyed with pleasure and you the one in control.

Another thrilling thing to do is for one of you to give the other a shampoo. This is a very sensuous experience, if done right, and its effects are even headier (pardon the pun) than a scalp massage.

Obviously, this is best done in a shower, but if you're not ready to get naked with this person, save it for another time. Use a shampoo that makes the scalp tingle, such as one with peppermint oil, to further enhance the experience. Or, use a shampoo with a tantalizing scent. Take your time rubbing in the shampoo. Deeply massage the scalp. Play with the hair, lifting it into peaks and swirls. The scalp is virtually alive with sensitive nerve endings. This is the most intimate place you can touch another person and not have it be obscene. Revel in the pure sensuality of a shampoo experience, whether you're the one giving or getting!

THE ART OF THE FLIRTY BATH

Taking a bath with someone is very sexy. While the main goal of a regular, everyday bath is to get clean, the object of a flirty bath is to get sexy! There's no room in the flirty bath for shaving, exfoliating, or whatever other grooming you need to do—if you're involved in a flirty bath, you should have done all of that already. Men really love to caress a woman's silky smooth, hairless leg, but they don't like to think too much about how it got that way.

The point of the flirty bath is to enhance intimacy. Besides, baths are even sexier when done in tandem!

Bath Buddies

Who you decide to take a bath with is up to your discretion. Of course, if you've already gotten pretty intimate, the tub is just another place to get to know each other better. But when you take a bath with a guy you don't know all that well, it could be really fun—or horribly awkward. While any guy gets excited by the idea of sharing a tub with a woman, at the same time he's bound to be a bit nervous because of the shrivel factor! No worries, though. After he gets a good look at your wet and rosy breasts floating in the water, usually that changes the situation pretty fast.

Supplies

Ideally, you'd be bathing in a great old-fashioned six-foot-long claw-foot tub overflowing with oodles of bubble. Or if you're a minimalist, a deep Japanese teak soaking tub. But in reality, you've probably got a run-of-the mill, all-purpose tub that will accommodate two people—even if it takes a little fancy maneuvering. That's why taking a bath with someone in a special place, like a hotel room, is really a treat. If you're away somewhere on a romantic vacation or weekend getaway with your boyfriend, definitely take advantage of any fabulous bathtub you encounter. In fact, plan on spending a long time in the water as foreplay. It's very flirtatious!

But even without the romantic fantasy getaway weekend for two, you can create a flirty atmosphere right in your own home. You've already got the guy, the tub, and the hot water, right? So throw in a couple of superfluffy (and hopefully clean) towels, tons of bubbles, and a little candlelight, and you've got yourself the ultimate Flirty Bath setting.

Bath Music for Two

Aside from the dulcet sounds of two people splashing, a little music goes a long way toward enhancing your Flirty Bath experience. No matter what your music preference, try to choose something that's smooth and comforting. Your guy may love Metallica, but that doesn't exactly make for a flirtatious bath experience. In the bathroom try some jazz or even a little classical music. Songs without lyrics usually work best, as they are less distracting.

Aromatherapy

Scent is the strongest of all the senses, so it doesn't hurt to throw a little aromatherapy into the bathtub mix. Like the music, try to pick a scent that's subtle and relaxing. Avoid anything particularly bracing, like wintergreen. Ditto for anything distinctly musky or heavy that will only be intensified by the hot water. Stick with light floral scents—they're calming and restorative without being cloying. Try scents like lilac and vanilla. If you wear a light perfume, try spritzing a few drops of your favorite cologne into the water while the tub is filling. Go easy on the amount. Steam amplifies scent.

Getting In

This may seem silly, but how you get into the tub can set the mood for the whole Flirty Bath experience. If you're trying to keep it on the light, playful side, get in first and make sure you look inviting—after all, it's pretty adorable to be covered up to the neck in bubble bath.

If you're going for the Sex Goddess angle, make sure you're the last one in—that way he has a chance to really ogle you as you're disrobing. Don't rush! Be proud of your body.

Scrub a Dub—Flirty Bath Activities

So you've got the mood, the candles, the music—now what? Don't worry your flirty little head. There's plenty to do when you're sharing a tub. You can wash each other's feet, you can wash each other's backs . . . or anything else you see fit to wash!

There are basically two positions you can assume with another person in the tub:

1. Facing each other
2. Lying back against the other person's chest

Both positions have their advantages. When you're facing each other, conversation is easy and you can see each other's eyes. You can toy with each other's feet. If you sit with your back to him and lean against his chest he can easily toy with your breasts. Here's an easy, sweet thing to do together in the tub: Read something aloud to each other. What about some love poetry?

Getting Out

Your fun doesn't have to end just because your bath does. Getting out of the tub is yet another opportunity for flirtatious fun, you just have to reach out and grab it (ha, ha). Offer to dry him off—and when you're finished, let him dry you.

Bathing in the Great Outdoors

Not all bathing opportunities happen inside the house, or in a hotel or motel room. Or even in a bathtub! It can be a lot of fun to take an outdoor shower with another person, say, if you're on a camping trip. You might even really be dirty. There's all that running water and you're standing straight up. Think on your feet and flirtatiously offer to wash his back and then ask him to return the favor! It's even more fun to shower together under a real waterfall. A trip to Hawaii, anyone?

HOT TUB

DOS AND DON'TS

Here are the most important hot tub and Jacuzzi etiquette tips!

- ❍ DON'T hog the bubbles.
- ❍ DO stay submerged. Your head and neck and the top of your chest should be the only flesh that shows!
- ❍ DON'T stay on your side of the tub. What is the point?
- ❍ DO ask if the other person is warm enough. Add more hot water as needed or push the temperature up.
- ❍ DON'T splash. The hot tub is not the ocean.
- ❍ DO have a pile of nice, clean, fluffy towels waiting when you get out.
- ❍ DON'T just stand there naked unless the other person is standing there naked, too.
- ❍ DO not act like you're in a seduction situation unless he initiates seductive action. Hot tubs are supposed to be playful, so keep the atmosphere light.
- ❍ DON'T get into any heavy conversations. Again, keep it light.
- ❍ DO play footsies under the water if the situation seems right!
- ❍ DON'T drink a lot of alcohol. People have been known to pass out in hot tubs.
- ❍ DO invite other people in (assuming this is a hot tub and not a Jacuzzi). When it comes to outdoor spas, the rule is, "the more, the merrier!"

The Hot Tub Flirt

Ah, the pièce de résistance of the Flirty Bath! It's impossible not to feel more relaxed when you're enveloped in steaming, churning water. Hot tubs stimulate the body's nerves and circulatory system, and they help relieve pain from arthritis, and neck and back problems, along with other muscle related ailments. If you have a martini in your hand while you're in a hot tub, so much the better. Picture this: It's a beautiful night. There is a tiny nip in the air. But it's nice and warm in the hot tub, where you've got the magic and the moonlight and maybe a couple of shots of Powers Irish Whiskey just off to one side. You could just lie back and gaze together at the stars. That's pretty flirtatious!

If you haven't got a hot tub, a Jacuzzi will do.

If you haven't got a Jacuzzi, God bless you.

BEACH . . . BLANKET—BINGO!

You're with your boyfriend and you're lying out on the beach. Unless you're the kind of gal who gets really cranky unless she's got her own towel space, chances are the two of you are sharing a blanket. You're both three-quarters naked and in super close proximity. This could be fun!

There is really no situation fraught with flirtatious expectations more than an afternoon at the beach. Okay, so not everyone has unlimited beach access, but it's really primo flirting real estate.

The combination of fresh air, sun, and sand is enough to make anyone feel a bit randy. To date no scientific evidence exists proving that salt air makes people horny, but unscientifically, it's a *very* flirty location. Maybe it's the heat or the smooth firmness of sand underneath you that seamlessly conforms to your body. If you're already lying on a blanket next to someone you think is special, you're halfway to nirvana.

YOU'RE ALL ALONE ON THE BEACH?
NOT FOR LONG!

So you didn't bring a Flirt Object of your own to the beach—does that mean you should miss out on all the fun? Just remember, a creative flirt girl can always conjure up a good Flirt Object!

- Lie on your stomach wearing dark sunglasses and surreptitiously let your eyes take in the full scene. Pick out a likely Flirt Object. Try not to pick someone else's boyfriend or beach date—that's just plain mean.
- If no likely objects appear on the horizon, relocate! Carry your blanket to another part of the beach. You never know—you might find the perfect Flirt Object just down the strand.
- When you've fixed your eye on someone worth taking a chance to flirt with, eyeball him. Make your gaze intense—keep noticing him until he notices you.
- As soon as he looks back, look away.
- Do this about six times over the next twenty minutes.
- If he won't play, give up.
- If he will play, mouth the words, "Come here."
- When he comes over to your blanket/chair (and trust me, he will), invite him to sit down.
- Say something simple and blatantly obvious, like, "How often do you come here?" Don't deliver your words coyly. Ask the question in a friendly but neutral tone. You want to come off as a flirt, not a hooker!
- Talk to him long enough to make sure he's not a creep. There are loads of jerks at the beach—so beware.
- If you've decided to ditch him as fast as you can (think of the whole experience as fishing, and in this case you've decided to throw your fish back), fib and tell him you have to go. Gather up your stuff, and refuse any offers he makes to help you haul your stuff to your car. If you have the misfortune to run into him later at the refreshment stand, act like you never saw him. This is not flirting. This is antiflirting. Think of it as flirting in reverse!

12 TIPS TO HAVING A BETTER TIME WITH YOUR GUY ON THE BEACH

1. Untie or unclasp your bathing suit straps. Sit up prettily while you undo them. It looks to a man like you're getting undressed. Which, in a way, you are!

2. At first, lie on your stomach and bury your head in your arms. This gives your blanket-mate carte blanche to study the back of your legs and your behind. Since you're not looking (feigning sleep is a good idea), he can just stare.

3. Flip over on your back after fifteen minutes. (In fact, flip over every fifteen minutes anyway to ensure an even tan.) The commotion of your motion and your nearly naked state will stir him into a frenzy. Plus, it will periodically give him new body parts to look at, which will keep his attention.

    While on your back, put a hat or a pretty scarf over your face. Trust me, there is nothing sexier than a nearly naked woman with her face covered up. It is a very erotic image. It has the same psychological (read: kinky) impact on a man as seeing a naked woman wearing a blindfold.

4. Ask your beach bud to put sunblock on you. Usually you start with asking him to do your back, but after that, it's up to you to tell him exactly where you want him to put it (oooh, do I hear a double-entendre here?). I suggest you ask him to anoint the back of your thighs.

5. Offer to put sunblock on him, too, but don't grope him! You want to seem friendly and helpful, not like a horny beast—unless, of course, that is the image you're hoping to project. Stick with the shoulders. You can knead a man's shoulders for a long, long time. When he starts purring like a big pussycat, you'll know you've hit a nerve.

6. Don't be the one to offer to get cold drinks or ice cream. Let him wait on you! You may suggest, however, that a cold drink would be a good thing to have just now. It is very flirtatious to put out hints.

7. When he returns with the refreshments, make sure you're sitting up on the blanket, maybe applying protective lip gloss or rubbing lotion on your arms. (Both these movements look sexy to a man.) Give him something good to look at as he's trudging his way toward you. Flash him your sexiest smile as he hands you your drink or cone. Behave as though he's just given you the most sought-after treat in the world.

8. Run into the ocean together. Have a race.

9. Jump the waves together. This provides lots of opportunity for touching and splashing.

10. Speaking of splashing—is there anything flirtier to do in the water? Splash him playfully and see how he reacts. You can learn a lot from a playful splash. If he's a fun flirt for you, or it seems like the relationship might actually go somewhere, he'll respond playfully and soon the two of you may even be smooching! If he gets mad or seems irritated, you'll know that he's not the guy for you. If this happens, the good news is you can stop flirting with him and begin flirting with someone else immediately!

11. Stroll down the beach together. Bump your hip against his a little. Make it seem like an accident.

12. At the end of the day, employ his help in shaking out the blanket and folding it up. You take one end, he takes his, you slowly walk toward each other . . . you get the picture.

FOOD FLIRTATIONS

At the great Greek and Roman orgies, beautiful women were given the job of hand feeding the bigwigs and the warriors, pressing juicy figs into the men's mouths and pouring wine down their gullets. Those folks really understood the concept of "party"! This is what spawned the great expression, "Peel me a grape!" You don't have to be a temple love goddess or curvaceous concubine to incite sexy feelings in a man through hand feeding. Even if you've never done it yourself, refer to some classic scenes in movies where couples hand feeding each other was subliminal sex. What about that wonderful scene in the movie *Tom Jones*, where he and this woman are seducing each other through food? True, it does get a little bit eighteenth-century slovenly, but it is a classic scene of food seduction on film!

Flirty Finger Foods

Why are finger foods flirty? Because they allow you to bring attention to your mouth. They're also flirty because if you use them right, you'll have the Object of Your Flirtation eating out of your hand—literally!

Chocolate is a meltingly sexy finger food to play with. As every sentient being knows, chocolate is anything but a kiddie treat. In reality it is a potent, druglike substance containing more than 300 known chemicals including the stimulant theobromine, the amphetamine phenylethylamine, and caffeine, another obvious stimulant. Chocolate is also chock-full of something known as xanthene derivatives, which increase endorphins, the brain's natural opiate.

Chocolate is an ideal flirtation food (read: aphrodisiac) because of the way it works on the body's neurochemistry. A controversial study conducted by researchers at the Neurosciences Institute in San Diego, California, revealed that chocolate contains pharmacologically active substances that have the same effect on the brain as marijuana. In fact, it may be those very substances that are responsible for certain drug-induced psychoses associated with cravings for chocolate. When you eat it, it induces warm and fuzzy feelings, which are definitely flirtatious!

What's the old saying? "Life is uncertain—eat dessert first"?

Other delightful finger foods that should be high on your flirt list include

-----> Strawberries
-----> Raspberries
-----> Slices of melon
-----> Grapes
-----> Shelled nuts (avoid ones dusted with salt unless you like flirting with the possibility of high blood pressure)
-----> Oysters on the half shell can be gently tipped into a Flirt Object's waiting mouth. As it turns out, oysters are also a known aphrodisiac. Why? It's because of their high zinc content, which has been clinically proven to improve sex drive!

> Feed your man with your hands. Spaghetti goes down much more amusingly if you eschew using forks. Gummy bears are fun, too!

> Lick that wisp of whipped cream off your guy's mouth.

> Share a jar of peanut butter. It's more than okay to use the same spoon.

> Go to the diner and order one milkshake with two straws. Sit side by side instead of across from each other in the booth and play footsies under the table as you enjoy your sweet treat.

> Take turns biting into an apple. One apple. Two people.

> Share an ice cream cone together. When it's your turn, take very emphatic licks.

PART THREE
putting it *all* together

CHAPTER 10

WHO WANTS TO BE THE BEARD?

Frame *bold* ideas— and then *hide* them.

Right now, you're probably saying WHAT?? A beard is facial hair sprouting out of someone's cheeks and chin! What the heck does that have to do with flirting?

Well, slow down, cowgirl! A beard is also a disguise. Think about it. On a man, a healthy beard can disguise a weak chin. It's this disguise element that gives the slang term *beard* its meaning. In matters of flirtation and romance (not to mention sexual intrigue), the role of the beard is to make other people believe that two people are "together," when in fact one of them has something going with somebody else. In modern flirting, a beard doesn't just have to be someone who is masquerading as your boyfriend (or girlfriend, if you're feeling frisky). No way!

The original bard, Shakespeare, talked about beards in his plays. *Twelfth Night* has so many jokes about beards it's nearly impossible to sort them out unless you're a Shakespearean scholar. Today, the word *beard* has a slightly different connotation. It's still a person who provides a disguise, but that disguise can take on different meanings. You can use a beard to get closer to the Object of Your Flirtation in many situations. Your beard could be a party host, a wingman (or woman), or even your own Secret Flirtation Partner.

HELLO, STRANGER

In your Flirt World, swinging an introduction to the Object of Your Flirtation can be darn tricky. Enter the Host Beard. With this beard by your side, you'll be able to get close to your man and work your magic much more quickly than you might have on your own.

Imagine you're at a crowded party and you're ready for fun. Your green light is on, you're wearing your flirt skirt, and you feel confident and fabulous. Far across the room, you spy a guy—your first Flirt Prospect of the night. Maybe he's drop-dead gorgeous. Maybe he just looks interesting. Maybe you just like his glasses. Or—maybe he's a celebrity. Whatever. You just want to take a crack at him, see if there's any flirt action you can get going.

So how do you get him to notice you without coming on too strong? You use a beard, of course! The most obvious beard in this situation would be the host or hostess. After all, it is his or her job to make you feel comfortable at their party—so get the host to wrangle you an intro. It's so much more subtle and interesting than hanging out by the bean dip all night and hoping he'll get hungry. Using the host as a beard is just one of many ways the beard system works.

IGNORE THAT MAN . . . SORT OF

Sometimes, the best way to get a man's attention is to not pay him any attention at all! Instead, focus on someone closer to you. Here's a hint: If you strike up a conversation with the woman right next to you, you can let her become your beard. This move is a guaranteed attention grabber.

Deep down, men are pretty nosy. They pay attention when two attractive women begin interacting with each other in an animated way. They'll stop what they're doing. They listen. They look. When a man sees two women together, a primal urge comes over him. They want to get right in on it, find out what the women are all about. Maybe it's because of the very common fantasy of having two women at the same time. It's an animal nature thing. Or so he thinks. Once you understand the animal nature of this situation, you can see for yourself why nothing lures a man to your side faster than having him see you flirt up another woman.

Here's how to do it:

1. Approach a woman who interests you—if she's someone you already know, all the better. If you don't know her, you can approach her by finding something to compliment her on— shoes, hair, handbag.
2. Keep the conversation light and friendly. The entire time you're talking, occasionally cast your eye in the man's direction.
3. Let your body language send him a message. Tell him that you've created a situation where he gets to talk to not just one, but two, interesting and attractive ladies.
4. When he walks over (and you can be sure he will), segue him into the conversation smoothly by asking him a cute question. Introduce your new friend. This is the beginning of what's called a Three-Way Flirt. But we'll get to that in detail in Chapter 11.
5. Now's your chance to show him you're interested, so this is where your stellar verbal flirtation skills must kick in—charm him, charm him, charm him!

6. Don't forget your beard! That would be rude. Be sure to direct questions back to her as well. Even though you're after the guy, flirting is all about making friends—with everyone. Just because you've lured your guy in doesn't mean you can drop your beard like a hot potato. By keeping everyone involved in the conversation, you become the flirt choreographer—the lady in control.

7. After a few minutes, invite him to come along with you to another location at the party—to refresh a drink, meet another friend, or maybe grab one of those canapés. If you've done your job, he'll follow along, just like a puppy dog.

8. Say goodbye nicely to that other woman. She's served her purpose and it's time to let her move on so she can find her own Flirt Object.

NUEVO BEARDS—AKA, WINGWOMEN

If you're a dedicated dater and flirter, you're well aware of the terms wingman, and wingwoman by now. In fact, the tactic covered in the last section is a form of using a wingwoman (even if she didn't know that's what she was).

A wingman is the most modern version of a beard and the newest twist to the Date and Mate scene. Wingwomen have gotten lots of attention from the press in the past year—you can't open the style section of most metropolitan daily newspapers without reading an article on this phenomenon. You can use your wingwoman or wingman to help you meet new men. They are your club-hopping buddy.

Making the Most of Your Wingwoman

The purpose of a wingwoman is to give you someone to riff with, to play off, while you're out on the town. Partly she's there to keep you company, but she's also there to help you look good. Your wingwoman could be a real buddy, even your best friend—or she could just be an attractive woman who looks good standing beside you, like in the last example. Here's how to work it with your wingwoman:

1. Make sure you prominently position yourselves in a guy's view, preferably within earshot.
2. Gossip together about anything that's going on in the room. Men claim to hate gossip, but most can't resist it.
3. Compliment her outfit and tell her how fabulous she looks. If she's a true wingwoman, she'll compliment yours back. This helps call out to any eavesdropping man what you're wearing. He'll look.
4. Flirt with her a little bit. Flirt behavior is contagious. It will rub off!

Making the Most of Your Wingman

Like a wingwoman, your wingman is a hot guy friend whose sole purpose is to help you find a fun Flirt Prospect. If he's dedicated to his job and to you, he'll help direct you to interesting, good-looking, dateable men. The benefit of having a wingman as opposed to a wingwoman is that you don't have to play it so coy. It's your wingman's job to make the initial approach. He's the one with the opening lines. He's in charge of the heavy lifting, the ice breaking, and he'll keep the conversation afloat so you can just jump in. In short, he's the warm-up act to your show. His mere presence makes you more interesting, maybe more appealing, and certainly gets the attention of other men.

Here's what a good wingman knows:

--→ He is there to showcase you. When you enter the room, he stays at your side. He takes off your coat, and he creates a bit of commotion so all eyes are on you.

--→ He should be at your side no matter what. He brings you drinks and the scoop on the most likely Flirt Prospects.

--→ His job is to make sure he gets you and your Flirt Prospect engaged in a conversation, and he is committed to this goal.

--→ His job is to keep the ball rolling until you and the prospect are fine on your own.

FLIRTING IN PLAIN SIGHT

Flirting in plain sight without anyone being the wiser is a true art and a carefully acquired skill. There are tools you can use to become better at it, and this is a perfect case of practice makes perfect! Try the tips in this section to obscure your most outrageous public flirting so that no one around you is the wiser—and nobody goes home later to gossip on the telephone about What Is Going On with You?

But why, you ask, would you want to flirt secretly in the first place? There are many circumstances that warrant flirting in secret, which we'll discuss shortly. The most important thing to know, however, is that it is just plain sexy. This type of flirting throws off so many sparks that it could start a giant fire! It's so much fun to flirt secretly in public that you absolutely owe it to yourself to try. How can you resist?

Now, back to the why of secret flirtation. Maybe the man you are flirting with is spoken for and his wife/girlfriend is intolerant of random flirts. This calls for some surreptitious flirtation. Or, maybe you just don't want to flirt openly because you want to avoid being the subject of gossip, for whatever reason.

Other circumstances can also call for secret flirtation. If you are at a professional function, you don't want to sully your reputation by being perceived as a tawdry flirt. You want to be recognized by your colleagues for your business savvy, not your feminine wiles. A woman has to come across as refined and well-bred to flirt well in a social situation like this. Your tactics must be cool and subtle. The flirt itself has to be cool and subtle. You need to keep things light—or at least make it look that way. It would be awful to have your reputation smudged or besmirched, and it might even cost you your job!

People flirt illicitly in public all the time. What do you suppose was going on with Bill Clinton and Monica? The "danger factor" of secret flirting—the risk of being caught—is exactly what makes it so appealing.

Follow these tips and guidelines to have fun but not get caught!

Avoid the Look of Love

Never, ever look as though you're in love with the Object of your Flirtation. How are

One problem with beards is that sometimes they want your man. How do you tell if your beard is deviously trying to hone in on your action instead of help you out? Here are some handy tips:

- She is laughing way too much at your Flirt Prospect's jokes.

- She's making physical contact with your quarry—playfully laying her hand on his arm, and giving him playful pokes.

- She not only asks for the Flirt Prospect's business card, but she asks for his cell number, too.

- When you come back from the bathroom, your beard is sitting in your Flirt Prospect's lap.

you going to keep things secret if you're going ga-ga over him in the middle of the party?

Covert Moves for Flirting in High-Risk Situations

Dare to flirt in a public place with someone you love, or even have a bad crush on, and, trust me, *everybody* will notice, even people who don't even know you! So here's the trick. Never look into that person's eyes. Normally that's a primary method of flirting, but if you're trying to keep it covert, avoid eye contact, or you'll be in danger of going from covert to overt! But if you're already in love, you must avoid it! Either what you see will melt you, or something will make you giggle or freak, and then you'll really be in trouble, trust me.

Armed and Dangerous

During a covert flirt, it's permissible to take his arm, but not his hand. An arm can provide you with friendly support and balance. But a hand—especially the thumbs and fingertips—is dangerous territory if you're trying to keep it low key. There's an ancient belief that the pulse of the thumb is directly connected to the pulse of the beating heart. With the hand and the heart connected, any touching between them is *tres intime.*

Think about the days of King Arthur's court, during the time of knights and ladies in waiting. Those men and women worked hard at perfecting the art of flirting in secret but in plain sight. Getting caught would have cost them their heads! Remember most of those ladies were married, most of the time to lords. That didn't stop some of them from flirting with the young swains, though. After all, this *was* the heyday of courtly love! A knight (always a dashing figure) could offer a lady his arm to help her cross a room (no mean feat in those enormous skirts and stiff corsetry), but their hot hands could only meet in the formal setting of a dance. So watch your hands . . . unless you are very, very sneaky.

Introductions . . . Please?

You are at a party. Much to your delight, one of your favorite Flirtation Objects shows up . . . with another woman. Could she be his girlfriend? If you're feeling dangerous, you can rattle his cage by pretending to your hostess that you don't know him and ask her to introduce you. Demurely pretend that you've never met—and definitely shake the other woman's hand!

Silence Is Worth a Thousand Words

There will be times when you're so overcome with desire for some guy who you've been flirting with that you're rendered speechless. All the clever lines you painstakingly came up with to use on your Flirtation Object are immediately wiped from your memory by the sheer power of hormones. Men, for some reason, find dumbstruck muteness in a woman incredibly attractive. Knowing this, you can fake it.

> "When I'm feeling overwhelmed with want, I practically can't speak. For some reason this is very attractive to some men and they'll practically stand on their heads to get me to say anything. I like playing this game."
> —*Roxanne*

Subtle Splendor

Express yourself in nontouching but intimate ways. For example, almost never look at him. Don't let any of your body parts touch. Do something totally subtle like rest your cell phones together. Just because you can't be close, doesn't mean your equipment can't be. Hey, he might be the one initiating a flirt with *you!* If he leaves his hat right next to your pocketbook, that can't be an accident.

ARE YOU A FLIRT ADDICT?

The following is a little psychological quiz designed to help you determine whether or not you are a Flirt Addict. Remember, there are no right or wrong answers. You're just trying to figure out how dependent on the flirtatious life-style you really are!

1. Aside from when you're PMS-ing, how often do you flirt?
   A. I flirt at bars or parties and only when I'm dressed up.
   B. I flirt with every cute guy I meet who isn't wearing a wedding band.
   C. I only flirt online when I can be anonymous.
   D. I've been known to flirt with dogs.

2. TRUE or FALSE: When I meet someone for the first time who gets my blood moving, I always touch some part of his body before I take my leave.

3. How many times a day do you use your cell phone for something other than confirming appointments or doing real business?
   A. Always
   B. Sometimes
   C. Never
   D. Business calls? What are those?

4. Would your closest friends (not to mention your enemies) describe you as a hopeless and incorrigible flirt?
   A. Yes
   B. No

5. Have you ever left the house without checking yourself out in a mirror?

A. No
B. Yes
C. Are you kidding?

6. **TRUE** or **FALSE:** I flirt with my friend's/sister's/mother's boyfriend or husband as a matter of course.

7. Have you ever flirted at a job interview?
   A. I have never flirted at a job interview.
   B. I have never not flirted at a job interview.
   C. Doesn't everyone flirt at job interviews? How else are you supposed to get a job?

8. If you're at a party and there's no guest you consider flirt worthy, what do you do?
   A. I flirt with the male wait staff.
   B. I flirt with another woman.
   C. I leave the party.

9. When shopping for a new car, how much do you factor in how you'll look driving it as opposed to your real car needs?
   A. None. I purchase cars for their value.
   B. A little. A cute car attracts cute guys.
   C. *Puh-leese!* My only concern is how I'll look driving it.

10. **TRUE** or **FALSE:** Given the choice, you would rather flirt than eat.

INTERPRETING YOUR RESPONSE:

1. If you answered:
   A. You're probably only a part-time flirt.
   B. You're a purposeful flirt, which means you're a sensible person with solid priorities in your head.
   C. You are a shy flirter, but all is not lost—there are plenty of covert flirting options available to you.
   D. You are truly a flirt addict. Congratulations! You should win a prize!

2. If you answered:

ARE YOU A FLIRT ADDICT?

TRUE: You've a very accomplished flirt. An expert flirter never underestimates the power of touch. There's electricity in them there fingertips—it's up to you to light the spark!

FALSE: If this is a move you've never used before—try it! You'll be surprised by the positive effect.

3. No matter what you answered—always use your cell phone for flirting, especially flirting during business hours, but only if it's frisky business!

4. If you answered:

   A. The words *hopeless* and *incorrigible* are actually compliments. Be proud—you're well on your way.

   B. So maybe hopeless and incorrigible aren't your flirt style. Try for smart and savvy instead. You can work your flirt style any way you want to!

5. If you answered:

   A. Proceed to Chapter 3 immediately. Once you've finished, retake this quiz. Any woman who calls herself a flirt has some kind of mirror action going at all times. For cryin' out loud, how else can you tell if you've got lipstick on your teeth?

   B. Good for you! Any true flirter is never too far from a mirror.

   C. Uh-oh. Sounds like antiflirting behavior, for sure. Are you certain this is the book for you?

6. If you answered:

   TRUE: Of course you flirt with the boyfriends and husbands of your friends/sister/mother. Of course you're only joking, and anyway, didn't you learn to flirt in the first place from being daddy's girl?

   FALSE: Remember, all good flirts go to heaven, but expert flirts have more fun.

7. If you answered:

   A. While it is risky to out and out flirt at a job interview (darn those pesky rules and regulations regarding sexual harassment in the workplace), a teensy bit of flirting will definitely make you a memorable candidate. Just watch how many times you cross your legs in that short skirt, okay, baby?

B. Good for you. You keep your work life and your flirt life separate—a smart move from a savvy flirter.

C. Slow down there, cowgirl! There's a time and a place for everything. Sounds like you've got flirting in your blood but you need to smooth out your moves. Good thing you've got this handy guide to help you out!

8. If you answered:

A. A true flirt expert never flirts with the waitstaff—she simply moves on to the next fabulous party.

B. Ahhh, this is a sign of true flirt brilliance. Flirting with another woman is not only a handy way to refine your skills, but in the right situation, it can help you attract a worthy male prospect.

C. Good answer—now make sure you lend a helping hand to the girl who chose answer A!

9. If you answered:

A. What a smart consumer you are! Please reference answer C immediately to help you put a little more flirt in your life.

B. You know how to work your look, but you don't want to flaunt it. When you wanna look hot behind the wheel, you always go for the convertible. A little deuce coupe wins hands down every time.

C. When it comes to cars, worrying your adorably tousled head about gas mileage, braking systems, air bags is so Been There, Done That—you're only interested in the car's FF ability. Translation: Flirt Factor!

10. If you answered:

TRUE: Food? Food? Who needs to eat when there's a flirting opportunity at hand? You know how to maximize flirting at every opportunity.

FALSE: Okay, so nutrition is important, but so is flirting. Remember, food can be very flirty, so use it to your advantage!

WHAT YOU CAN LEARN
FROM CHEATING COUPLES

Cheaters, as you may well imagine, are experts at using beards to disguise what they're doing. Unless they're secretly dying to get caught, cheaters are usually great at hiding their relationship from prying, nosy eyes. While I'm not advocating that you take up with guys who are not truly available or start having illicit affairs, you can take a page from the cheater's handbook on how to conduct a flirtation that must be kept under wraps for one reason or another, or just for fun. (Just keep in mind, when a married man tells you how unhappily married he is, when he's got three kids at home, he's not leaving—trust me.) Here are the basic tricks:

- Meet in out of the way places, not where you go with your friends. Ask for a table in a corner. Sit with your back to the wall and keep an eye peeled on the door at all times. If someone you know walks in and sees you, be sure to acknowledge them. If necessary, introduce your tablemate as a business associate. Do whatever you can to quell suspicious minds.

- Avoid wearing perfume or stick with a highly popular scent. You don't want to mark the other person with your unique and highly memorable aroma.

- Get a restricted number for your cell phone. Make sure it's one that hides your name.

- Use instant messages to send love notes, not regular e-mail. Instant messages aren't automatically "saved."

- In public situations where you find yourselves together, be friendly but reserved. But if you're normally outgoing and gregarious, don't be too reserved! Your coolness will be duly noticed by sharp observers, and they will wonder why you're behaving differently.
- Limit use of your Love/Flirt Object's name. It's a dead give-away something's up when you can't stop talking about that person.

Cheaters *do* enjoy that special thrill that comes from engaging in high-risk activities. Borrow that energy and make it your own even if your budding romance is perfectly legitimate. Make up code names for each other and call your dates "assignations." Pretend you're a cheating couple even though you're not! Furtive behavior lends a hint of sauciness to every flirt relationship. Try doing more of it especially if your Flirt Object is your longtime boyfriend or even spouse. You never know. It might be just the thing to wake up your dull relationship!

• • •

Now that you've become an accomplished covert operations flirting specialist, it's time to move on to three-party flirting, or how to actively flirt with more than one person at a time.

CHAPTER 11

THREE-PARTY FLIRTING

Three is *not always* a crowd.

It really is easier to flirt with two men at once than one. Flirting with one guy at a time poses real challenges. For one thing, it means a girl really has to work it! Flirting with more than one guy at a time may sound like double effort, but in fact, it means you don't have to do much at all. Because of the genetic chemistry hard-wired in males, the guys will be in total competition with each other and they'll be fighting over you!

PROS OF THREE-PARTY FLIRTING

Three-party flirting has its pros, even though it may seem a little more labor intensive at first glance. It's a laid back, more casual form of flirting—you're still playing the field instead of committing to one Flirt Object, which is what you're doing when you use a beard.

When you're involved in a fun three-way flirt, you can relax and get a little creative with it. Think about it—when you're flirting with one guy, you've really got to concentrate! You have to focus. You have to be alert and make him feel special.

If you're flirting with two (or more!) guys, it takes the pressure off you and puts it on them. Their natural competitiveness and sexual jealousy takes over and keeps the action going. If you're lucky enough to find yourself in this position, sit back, relax, and enjoy the flirt.

Beard . . . or Bust?

You're probably thinking, what makes three-party flirting different from using a beard? Relax, woman! If you're still on your way to becoming a bona fide Flirt Expert, it may be difficult to see the difference between a beard and a three-party flirt.

It does get a bit complicated but once you get the hang of it, you'll see that the two couldn't be more different. Using a beard is all about commitment. When you're using a beard to meet a guy, you've got your sights set on one specific person. Your beard is playing a supporting role, helping you get closer to the Object of Your Flirtation. When you engage in three-party flirting, you're playing the field a little bit. You aren't focused on one guy in particular, but rather, you're using your charms to flirt up two guys at once.

THREE IS YOUR LUCKY NUMBER

Numerologists are really into the number three. Apparently it's very mystical. According to the lore of numerologists, in the manifestation of three, we find the condition of dynamic balance. The configuration of three always suggests movement from one aspect to the other while being fixed in between. In the language of numerology, three is often described as the essence of life itself. Say what? In laymen's language, what this means is that three is the most dynamic number, the one packed with energy. In a flirting scenario, three humans interacting basically triples the energy. If you doubt this, rent that movie *Jules et Jim*, which is all about one woman who spends all her time in Paris hanging out with two guys. Lots of flirting! You may be feeling a little more playful and adventurous. You're not committing to anyone in particular—you're exploring all of your options equally.

Common Three-Party Flirting Scenarios

So you've found yourself in the lucky position of flirting with two guys at once. They could be brothers. Or they could be buddies. Or they could be two guys who don't know each other from Adam who just happen to be standing next to each other at the bar. Your job is to flirt up both of them. Why? At this point you don't know which one of them is better.

There are a number of different scenarios where three-party flirting can be used. If you're out there on the flirt scene, you'll experience all of these scenarios sooner or later.

Guys have been spiking girls' drinks with ginger for centuries as a way to make them "hot." It's true that taken in small amounts, ginger does cause a bit of a flush, but imbibe too much of it and you'll be spending the night in the bathroom!

SCENARIO A: You never saw either of these guys before. They're both adorable and you wish you could know them, so you work your magic to flirt up both of them at the same time.

SCENARIO B: There are two guys, and you know one of them, but you've never met his friend. Guy One is fun to flirt with but for various reasons you've already ruled him out as a boyfriend. But what about the other guy? As a savvy flirter, you can work a three-party flirt to find out if his friend, Guy Two, is worth getting to know a little better.

SCENARIO C: You know both guys pretty well. You find them both attractive. They both find you attractive. Once you begin flirting with the two of them, you've incited a contest. Which guy will win? You pick!

THE NITTY GRITTY ON HOW TO FLIRT WITH MORE THAN ONE GUY AT A TIME

So how exactly do you flirt with more than one man at a time? Is it like trying to be in two places at once—a physical impossibility? Aside from sitting in the middle and holding a guy in each hand, how does a girl manage to keep two guys engaged and interested when there's only one of you? Following are some fail proof tricks for you to try.

Use Your Head

In order to flirt with multiple men, you've got to learn how to divide your attention. Therefore, how you use your head is of utmost importance. Think of your head as a spotlight, and you're shining it on whoever is doing the talking at the moment. That way, you appear to be enraptured with all of the men and you're making sure each is getting equal time and attention from you, which is of utmost importance.

Eye, Eye

Use your eyes! Follow the conversation with your eyes as though your two orbs were tennis balls. Be prepared for a fast and furious match. What if Guy One launches into a monologue on a topic you find utterly boring? You can use your eyes to break him out of his diatribe by flicking them quickly from one guy to another. This will give Guy Two an opportunity to jump in, or it could show Guy One that he's hogging the spotlight. And by now he should understand that there's only enough spotlight for one person—you! Whatever you do, don't keep your eyes on him for too long when he's speaking—this puts you in the dangerous position of:

A. Losing Guy Two because he thinks you're not interested
B. Getting stuck in a lengthy (read: boring) conversation with Guy One, causing you to miss out on numerous flirt opportunities

Use "Man Speak"

When you're entertaining several men at one time, chances are they're not going to want to hear about the new Japanese hair-straightening treatment you're dying to try. They don't want to hear gossip about movie stars. They don't enjoy talking about cellulite. The only way you're going to keep your multitude of men interested is by talking about the stuff that interests them. If you want to hang with the guys, you have to put on your man hat. Take stock of your group and try to stick to topics you think might interest them—sports, cars, boats, motorcycles, the stock market, and, of course—sex! Talking about sex is sexy. Bring up any sexy topic—poll them about what they think about Victoria's Secret mannequins being half naked in suburban store windows or ask how they feel about thongs—and you'll see. It's just a matter of winding 'em up and getting 'em going.

It's a porn film perennial, but men do love to see women eating and playing with ice cream cones, popsicles, or anything that involves a lotta tongue. Any food that is consumed by licking is very flirty. Men also get turned on watching any woman eat a food that remotely resembles a phallus. Bananas, for example, can be very flirty.

Let Them Do the Talking

Very often the best thing to say when in the company of two men is . . . nothing. If you can pull off the Silent and Beautiful act without seeming like you have nothing to say, go for it. Sometimes after they run out of steam talking about man stuff, the tide will turn and they'll begin talking about what's really important—you! How gorgeous you look. How mysterious you seem. Wondering out loud what it is that is running through your pretty little head. Could it be that you're thinking about *them?* If you think that Silent and Beautiful is a good route for you, then pay attention to these Dos:

DO keep your mouth shut when you have nothing in particular to say.

DO look attentive! Nod and appear as though you're following the conversation (remembering to keep eye contact with both of them).

DO paste an expression on your face that conveys utter fascination.

DO let them do most of the work. If you play the silent type, they'll work even harder to win your affections—let 'em!

So Many Men, So Little Time

Okay, so you started off in control of your three-way, but you suddenly realize that you're in great danger of losing one of your men—you've been paying too much attention to Guy One, which means Guy Two is being neglected. Perhaps you forgot the eye contact rule. Perhaps the conversation was interesting and you got a little distracted. When you're flirting up a couple of guys at the same time, it's common to get into a trouble spot such as this. If you've let it get this far, your three-party flirt is in terrible danger of stopping cold. What to do?

If you've spent the last twenty minutes praying Guy Two would bail anyway, this is your chance to give him the boot. Try any of these tactics:

⤏ Sweetly say, "I'm so sorry. It seems that Rafael and I have so much to talk about." At that point any guy with a shred of dignity will know when to walk away.

⤏ Exclusively direct all your conversation to the guy you like. Be really obvious.

⤏ Take out your cell phone and call someone—preferably someone you can flirt with! Bad cell phone etiquette should give him the signal pretty quickly.

⤏ Announce you have to leave. Invite Guy One to leave with you.

What about the one you want to keep? How do you make it clear you're interested?

Have no fear—here are some tips to keep him in the mix:

⤏ Work that body! Use your body language to convey to Guy Two that he has every reason to believe he should hang in there.

Touch him. Drape your arm around his neck. Rest your hand on his arm. Men understand physical. He'll get it.

---> Wink at him. This will let him know you're still interested, despite Guy One's lengthy story.

---> Throw in a comment that will help get the conversation back on even ground. This will help you regain control and let Guy One know that if there's any alpha dog in this situation—it's you.

A LITTLE HEALTHY COMPETITION

In case you haven't noticed, guys are incredibly competitive. Put two guys in a room—any two guys, friends, brothers, dads and grown sons, little boys, big boys—and you're bound to see them compete over just about anything. Try it for yourself. Put two guys next to each other and introduce something they can fight over (food, turf, women) and just watch the show begin. This is kind of crude, but in a way, men regard women as food and turf. If you can stand it, imagine yourself as a delicious sirloin steak being ogled by two carnivores, or as virgin land being viewed by competing real estate developers.

Crowding and Jostling for Position

Shoving matches and shouting contests are not unusual between men when they're both after the same thing. That's competition. Sometimes the way competition asserts itself is loud and obvious. But it also can be deceptive, subtle, and hard to read. Bizarrely enough, a guy might be not even be attracted to a woman, but as soon as he's in the company of someone who is, suddenly she's the most desirable thing in the world to him and he won't be happy until he wins her.

Get That Natural Competition Mojo Working for You

So by now, you see that handling a good three-party flirt comes down to understanding the competitive nature of males. That's ultimately what it's about. Primitive male position and dominance! In the presence of a woman, men will naturally compete with each other. Since they're going to compete no matter what, you might as well use this to your advantage. Here's how to keep them competing for your affections:

---> Be pretty. Act sexy. They're competing for a prize—you!
---> If you sense the competition is dying down and they're starting to bond (heaven forbid!), ratchet up the heat by acting a tiny bit more flirty to one of them. Works every time!
---> Grab their attention by doing something physical. If you're at the beach or a pool, ask one of them to put some suntan lotion on for you. If your goal is to create a feeding frenzy, ask both of them to help.
---> Create and use rivalry from a distance. Out of earshot from the other, tell one guy what the other one is doing for you—i.e., driving you to the mall, picking you up at the airport. Odds are the other guy will fall all over himself to offer his services. Use it! Get him to hang up those shelves you've always wanted, or better yet, get him to paint your living room! Flirt up a storm with whichever guy you're alone with at the time.

Did You Say "Tag Team"?

A really smart and flirtatious female, no matter what her age, quickly grasps that two males are an improvement over one. Even moderate attention from two males is often preferable to the full attention of one.

For example, when one guy becomes tiresome, you always have another guy to fall back on! Maybe alone neither of them has enough money to buy your drinks. But if the three of you go out together, they'll combine forces to cover your tab.

That's why smart women naturally gravitate toward situations that involve men in pairs or groups. Contrary to the idea that two men are likely to overpower a woman (although that can happen, more on that in a minute), many women intuitively grasp that there's safety in numbers and that spending time with two men is often far less risky (and labor intensive) than having to deal with one man at a time. A man alone is a lone wolf. Whether you want to think of him this way or not, the fact is, he's a predator.

Going out in a datelike or social situation with two men is a plus for a woman. It means she's got rivals who work at outdoing each other, each trying to prove he's the "better man." They will vie for the woman's attention, possibly showing her more consideration than either one might do if he and she were alone. Two men also serve the practical function of keeping each other in check: As long as they're not working together as a hunting team (and some men will do that), the presence of two men normally ensures that no woman gets grabbed, mauled, verbally abused, put in a situation of danger, or compromised. Two men can maintain standards of decency. Plus, if you're out with two men and one of them becomes incapacitated, you always have a backup man to rely on.

But watch out! Occasionally two men will overcome their sense of competition with each other and work together to try to conquer *you*. And that's not the kind of three-party flirting situation you intended.

FLIRTING IN THE COMPANY OF YOUR EX
(AKA, THE REVENGE FLIRT)

Sometimes it happens that you find yourself in the company of an ex. It could be an ex-husband, an ex-boyfriend, or just a guy you fooled around with. It happens. Most women, even when they live in big cities, inhabit a relatively small universe. They go to the same five restaurants over and over, hang out at the same coffee shop or bar. Unless a major breakup or significant job change precipitates your moving to another city entirely, your odds of running into somebody you dated, lived with, or were even married to are actually pretty good. When this happens, what should you do? Freak out? Or make the most of it?

Chances are your ex isn't exactly going to help you flirt with new guys. Because he can't have you, he doesn't want anyone else to! Don't even think about using an ex as a beard unless it was a very amiable breakup—or he's paying you steep alimony and the only way for him to get out of it is to get you married off as quickly as possible to somebody else.

Whether we admit it or not, it's always fun to get a little revenge on the ex. It is especially gratifying when you happen to run into him when you're looking fantastic and out with your new guy. Say you and your new man bump into your ex, even on the sidewalk. As a flirt expert, what do you say/do? Start with any one of these suggestions and take it from there:

⋯⋯> "Hi, Robert. You're looking not so well. Isn't anyone taking care of you? Have you met my friend Steve? Guess what? He's taking care of me now!"

⋯⋯> "Gosh, Sam. I heard a rumor that you'd lost your job. Is that true? Oh yeah, have you met my friend Jake? Yeah, he's a stockbroker. Doing really well for himself. Next week he's taking me to Aruba."

----> "Cameron! Long time no see! My mother told me she ran into your mother and your mom says you've moved in with her again!"

----> "Andy! How are you! Still driving that old beater? Oh yeah, those are my new wheels. They belong to my new boyfriend, Mike. Don't you just love Lamborghinis?"

GIRLFRIEND FLIRTING

We've been through just about every type of flirting, but we haven't talked about how your friends factor in to your flirtation situation. If they're willing and able, your girlfriends can be one of your biggest flirting resources. You just have to be sure your friend wants to be in on the game and be in synch with you. It's a simple concept, and you've probably used it before without even realizing it was a super flirtation tactic. What you are doing is using your girlfriend as a go-between.

Playing the Advocate

If your girlfriend already knows the Object of Your Flirtation well, this is great news for you! She can act as a spokeswoman on your behalf to let him know just how fantastic you are. Ask her to send him e-mails about you. Make sure she finds ways to keep dropping your name. Get her to use her investigative skills to find out who else he might be going out with, his availability. When you're not there (but she is) have her find ways to keep introducing something cool about you into conversation. If you've only just started to know him, have her instigate a bit of jealousy-curiosity by mentioning something you're doing with another guy.

If she's already his good buddy, ask her to have him join you the next time the two of you girls are getting together. Invite him to go with you skiing or to the movies. This gives you prime opportunity to work your flirting magic, and it gives your girlfriend the chance to give you flirt backup support. It's really a win-win situation!

Commitment Conundrum

If you and the guy have been casually dating for a while and you're wishing he would make some commitment, plan a lot of activities with your girlfriend and her love interest (if she has one). Prop them up in front of him as the perfect picture of coupleness. Go on a double date. A word of caution: If she's married and has a houseful of kids, don't bring your boyfriend over unless you and he are really serious. Deep matrimony and all those rug rats might scare the pants off him and he'll vamoose!

If your girlfriend isn't involved with anyone, no worries. You can create a perfect picture of coupleness *with your*

You really can use your best girlfriend to sweep a guy off his feet. Here's some specific things a top-shelf advocate does:

- She tells him all your good points—and leaves out the negative ones!

- She treats him like he's royalty, further underlining her great respect and love of you.

- She tells him little details particular to you, like your great fondness for pineapple pizza or your favorite bands.

- She offers to take him shopping to help him buy you a great gift.

- She repeatedly finds ways to let him know what a great catch you are and how lucky he is to have found you.

- She covers your back when you screw up. Like that time you said you had to stay home to give the dog a bath when you were really meeting your old boyfriend for one last powwow.

girlfriend. That's right. Make lots of plans together for dinner, movies, weekend road trips. If he's not that into you, then why should you spend your time chasing him? Hang out with your girlfriend and give him a chance to miss you a little.

There will be times that you will be caught up in a flirt threesome, only instead of two men, there will be two women. There are two ways this situation can pan out. The most obvious is that you and the other woman will be in competition with each other, which usually translates into the two of you going head to head in a contest of hair tossing, leg crossing, and skirt hiking. Your clever conversation and repartee may reach new and astounding heights. On the plus side, you get a chance to demonstrate your verbal prowess and your incredible wit and humor. On the downside your friend may have legs like a thoroughbred race-horse and *oooh-fah* cleavage that leaves your modest proportions in the shadows—that is, the shadows her breasts create.

The second possible scenario is that you and the other woman will work together, playing off each other to your mutual benefit. This is really the ideal situation, because you get to have some fun working the guy as a team—girl power!

Friends or Rivals?

This is a different twist on the tag team concept we've already covered—only this time, you're on the tag team.

What if you and another woman take a shine to the same guy? Rather than trying to outdo each other in a contest of Who's Sexier, work together with that woman to knock the man off his feet, or at least to leave him stunned and senseless. Together you can make a big fuss over him, and build him up. You can play Good Cop, Bad Cop with him. The two of you take turns playing the dual roles of "Naughty" and "Nice."

You're working together with the unspoken agreement that this is a rival situation and one of you ultimately may prove the victor. While one of you praises him to the hilt, the other finds something about him to pick on—and then you reverse roles. Naturally, when you do this, you aren't playing to win. The odds are that neither one of you is going to Get That Guy—at least not that evening. To flirt well with a man alongside another woman, there has to be some tacit agreement between the two of you that neither one of you is playing for keeps. Unless the game is that you're both going to go home with him for a real "threesome." That's called a *ménage à trois,* and it's a topic for another book altogether!

You're the Token Female in the Office

What if you work almost exclusively with men? This may sound like a dismal occupational sentence at first, but you just have to look at it from a flirtastic perspective—eight hours a day, five days a week, you have a bevy of guys with whom to work your flirting magic.

When you find yourself in this kind of situation, you have only two choices. You either:

1. Become "one of the guys" and blend in

    or

2. Learn to handle enormous amounts of testosterone with flair, and even get a kick out of it

If you can hold your own working alone in the company of men, you're a unique woman with a unique flirting opportunity. If you're good at quick repartee, working with men will give you the opportunity to sharpen your flirtatious tongue.

Working in an all-guy world is one of the best opportunities you'll have to really get inside the heads of men and figure out the quickest route to good flirtations. You've got to be able to handle ribald humor, off-color jokes, and the fact that when you visit the restroom, the toilet seat is probably up.

Okay, so it sounds a little dismal, but you can make the most of it. Instead of being their doormat (i.e., the one making the coffee every morning, doing clerical work that's not a part of your job responsibility), be their queen. Wouldn't you rather park your tushy on a pedestal and have them wait on you? Even if your job is to be the secretary to a group of executives and they're the ones with the big desks and salaries, while you're handling the phones and all the correspondence, seize control of the situation and carry yourself like a princess. It's all about your actions. If you act as though you think the world of yourself, amazingly, they will follow. Every group of guys secretly yearns for a Queen Bee to rule their hive, a Snow White to tend to their Seven Dwarfs. If you flirt with one man, flirt with them all. Be completely fair and equal in your dealings among them, but treat yourself best of all so they remember that *you are the one on top!*

Here are some tips for flirting with a big group of men—especially when they're your coworkers:

---> Remember office or work-related flirting must stay light and low key. It's fine to joke around by the water cooler, but going out to lunch with any one guy is verboten.

---> Let them wait on you. Don't you be the one in charge of the coffee maker!

---> Flirt with them equally or don't flirt with them at all. In this situation it could be disastrous to play favorites.

---⟩ Flirt enthusiastically but don't date anyone.

---⟩ What happens in the office stays in the office. No telling tales out of school.

QUEEN FLIRT OF THE CHATROOM

It's Friday night but you're too whipped to whip yourself into shape to go out. So you decide to take the lazy road and do your flirting at home, online. Men you meet online don't know that you're just getting over the flu and that you haven't washed your hair in a week. You've been chatting online for hours, and your clever lines and ability to type ninety-nine words a minute have gotten you loads of attention. Three guys are IMing you. How do you handle it?

Act Like He's the Only One

Stroke the guy's ego—let him believe that you are talking to him and him alone. After all this is all in good fun, so why ruin a good thing? Once you've got them alone, you can be anything you want to be—blond, redhead, brunette. To encourage the idea that you're only talking to Him, let your IMs get personal. No, you don't have to tell him your bra size! Instead, ask him specific questions, like what's his favorite kind of music or his favorite thing to eat. Do tell him a bunch of stuff about yourself— even if none of it is true. The biggest way to sustain the fantasy that you're talking to him and him alone is to repeatedly use his name. You'll probably have to ask him what it is. To be sure, his IM name, *Infidel107,* for example, isn't! Last but not least, allowing a guy to think you're talking only to him is incredibly flattering. The guy thinks he's got your full attention . . . even while you're wildly IMing three others.

Deciding to Be Alone with Him

One guy in the room sends you an IM. You've been happily chatting with lots of people in a chatroom, but now this one wants to be alone with you. Why? Nine times out of ten, the only reason he singled you out for a private chat is to try to score online sex. If you're interested in discussing what you look like in your bra, go ahead. Otherwise, let's see. Why would you decide to go into a private chat room with one guy when you've already got several men talking to you?

→ This one guy's conversation is a genuine stand out. The rest are just drips.

→ You need a break from the heavy lifting of multiple chattings. Face it, your head is starting to swim.

→ One of the several guys you've been talking to is beginning to freak you out, and you want to get the opinion of another guy in the room.

Three important tips on how to handle more than one IM partner at once:

1. Keep the flirt moving. Learn to type fast.
2. Try to talk to each of them about basically the same thing. That way you won't lose the thread of the conversation or mix each guy up.
3. Never let on that you're talking to more than one guy at a time even though you can pretty much expect that your IM partners are talking to more than one girl at a time!

CHAPTER 12

BEDROOM FLIRTING

When there's something you *want*
and *flirting* seems the
only way to get it,
pull out all the *stops*.

WHO WANTS WHO?

You've been flirting for days, weeks, or, in the speeded-up version, one really intense hour. You want to spend the night with him and you're pretty sure he wants to spend the night with you. What are some body language specifics you can use to signal him that you're ready for this to happen?

Use Your Mouth

But not for talking! This is a situation in which using explicit body language works best to let him know what you want. Put yourself right in front of him. Face to face. Step into his personal space as much as humanly possible without your bodies actually touching. Put your mouth near his. Really close—as close as you can get without kissing him. Tilt your head like you're about to be kissed. If you're playing the Shy Type, now's the time to close your eyes. If you're a bold adventurer, lock your eyes on his. Either way, he should make the next move!

Just Kiss Him, Already!

That's right—just go for it. Lay a big fat smacker right on his mouth. Take command of his body by pressing your body against his. If you're feeling bold, try pushing him against the couch if you have to. Then go to it—lock your lips on his. Make it a soul kiss, so he understands you're hot and serious.

Play the Tickle Game

Tickling is really hot and sexy. In some women, tickling alone has been known to produce orgasm! Most tickle moves address the middle of the body, the tummy and sides specifically. So get a little playful—it's a great way to get your hands on his body and show him how you feel about him. Now, if you let your tickling fingers roam further south . . . well, he will get the message!

Put His Hands on You

Nothing telegraphs a man that a woman is interested in sex faster than her taking him by the hand and placing it on an erogenous zone. Obviously you're showing him you mean business if you take his hand and place it on your breast or between your legs. And it will be a major turn-on for both of you. You can use this in conjunction with the tickling move if you like. When you're laughing and tickling and generally fooling around like puppies, this is a playful move, but it has serious implications. Don't use this move unless you mean business or you want to get a reputation as a tease.

Talk about Sex

You want him. You're going to get him. So stop beating around the bush and use verbal flirtation cues that will point that man in the right direction. Be specific! It's too embarrassing for a woman to think she's asking a guy for sex and he doesn't "get" it—you want to make sure he knows exactly what you're talking about. You've gotten this far, haven't you? It's understandable that you want to tell him without saying something like "I'm horny," although that works pretty well. In fact, it's an instant flag-raiser, if you get my drift. There are less crude ways for a woman to express her physical desires. Here are some verbal ways to close the deal.

1. Use Double-Entendres

"Would you like to come in?" means something different when you've spent the last half-hour mouth-wrestling on the couch than if you're standing outside the door to your apartment after a first date. In the second situation, all it means is, "Would you like to come inside my apartment and maybe have a cup of tea?" In this situation it means, "Would you like to make love to me?"

2. Be Ladylike but Direct

"I want you to make love to me," means the same thing as "Let's get it on." Beware though—a lot of guys freak when they even hear the word *love*. Love or lovemaking can signal commitment! If you suspect that is the case here, and you don't expect this guy to hand you an engagement ring just because you both took off your pants, tweak your language a bit and try saying, "I would really love to get in bed with you." It works.

3. Use Big Hints

Informing a guy you've been seeing that your roommates are all out of town, that you're all alone for the weekend, or in any way giving him the info that you've got twelve or fifteen hours to kill alone is as good as saying, "Come over tonight and make out with me." Unless you tell him that you've invited lots of people over for a party, he'll get the cue that what you're hoping for is a party for two.

4. Get a Little Raunchy

This kind of verbal action is definitely not for everyone. Only brazen and sexually sophisticated babes can usually pull this off. Telling a guy that he's made you wet or that your nipples are hard or that you want to taste him is a grown-up sport. This is hot talk and it gets a hot reaction. Make it a rule to not play around with this kind of talk unless you anticipate immediate action.

YOU'RE NOT SURE HE WANTS YOU

He's flirting back. He seems to like you. You think he's interested in pursuing a more physical relationship with you. He hasn't given you a single Stop sign or in any way indicated that he's gay or not interested in sex. But he hasn't really given you the green light, either. In short, you're hanging out with Hard to Read Guy. Before using your flirtatious tactics to find out if this is going anywhere, take stock first by reviewing this checklist of hints he might be sending you if he's ambivalent about sex:

- He kisses you for an hour but his hands stay in all the safe zones.
- One minute he's all hot and heavy and the next he's calm as a lake. What's it all mean? It means he's ambivalent!
- In the middle of a hot make-out session he suddenly starts talking. Bad sign!
- He's told you on more than one occasion that you remind him of his sister.

20 KILLER LINES
YOU SHOULD MEMORIZE RIGHT NOW

1. Got a light?
2. Need a light?
3. My name is—. And, you are?
4. This party is pretty boring.
5. This party is excellent! Aren't you just loving it?
6. Where's your wife?
7. My boyfriend couldn't make it. I'm here all alone.
8. Nice tie.
9. Nice pants.
10. Nice shoes.
11. Hey! I have that sweater!
12. I see that you like to shop. Or did your girlfriend pick out your outfit?
13. My ride just bailed on me.
14. You said you worked where?
15. I've always wanted to meet (a cop, a fireman, a reinsurance strategist).
16. How clever of you to think of that. Would you repeat what you just said?
17. Your brother and my mother went to school together. Ha, ha, only kidding!
18. I'm just exhausted. Do you think we could go somewhere that's quiet?
19. I've never laughed so hard at a joke in my life. Tell another, quickly.
20. Do you ride?

→ When you say goodbye, he shakes your hand instead of giving you a hug and a kiss

Are We Going to Do It or Not?

Right this moment things seem pretty hot and headed in a boudoir direction, but so far nothing totally conclusive has happened to say the deal is sealed. How can you ask for sex in a way that makes it seem that you're not really asking—just in case you get rejected? Here are some physical and verbal tips to help you establish where your relationship is going:

→ Say, "I haven't had sex in a long time. What about you?" This tells a guy sex is on your mind but that you don't have a definite game plan.

→ Lick his earlobe and moan a little. If he pulls you toward him in a passionate embrace, the problem is solved, no problem. If he responds very slowly and just continues to kiss and fondle you, it isn't a foregone conclusion that you're going to be in bed with him soon.

→ Whisper in his ear that you're feeling kind of naughty. This should either kick off a round of flirty dirty-talk leading to the removal of your clothes, or exactly the opposite. If he fixes his glasses back on his head and starts interrogating you about what exactly you mean by the word *naughty*, forget it. He's not going to have sex with you.

→ Sit on his lap. If his arms don't wrap around you and you don't feel his manhood firming up, give him a friendly peck on his cheek, get off his lap, and see about what's for dinner.

→ Do a little striptease for him. Take off your shirt and toss it at his head. If he tosses it back at you, act as though nothing unusual has happened and get dressed. Just so you don't feel like a total fool, hum a few bars of striptease music as you fasten your buttons or fluff your hair. Make it seem like your impromptu dance was just part of your natural joie de vivre and not an overt sexual invitation that got nixed.

⋯⋯→ Say the P word. As soon as you start talking about your privates, you'll find out soon enough if he's curious to explore them.

How to Tell if He Wants You: Me, Tarzan—You, Jane

Guys are pretty direct in how they go about telling you they want you. They're not ones to beat around the bush—no pun intended. Men, primitive creatures that they are, tend to use simple, nearly caveman language and bestial gestures to communicate their needs. They don't pussyfoot. They don't equivocate. If a guy wants you, there's nothing much for you to figure out other than, Do you want him? So how will you know for sure that what he wants more than anything is to jump all over your body and be hooked up with you for hours? Here's some tips:

⋯⋯→ Male animals express their interest in mating by sniffing and licking the female's anatomy. A guy who is licking any part of your body, including your newly pedicured feet, clearly wants to eat you. But if he's just inhaling and exclaiming over that magical Calypso perfume you've so generously anointed yourself with, don't expect raw action.

⋯⋯→ He grabs you by the waist and basically carries you over to the sofa. Help him out by not going limp like dead weight. After all, you don't want him wrenching his back!

⋯⋯→ He says overtly sexual things to you, like "I'd like to tear your panties off." There's no mistaking the message in that.

ARE YOU SURE
YOU'RE READY?

You think you're ready, but are you? Remember, sex is an irrevocable experience, even the most casual sex. Once you've done it with a guy, you've done it. You won't forget it—even if sometimes you want to! Before doing anything you're really not ready for, ask yourself the following questions:

- Am I only going through with this because I've invested nineteen hours in flirting with him and there has to be some payoff?

- Do I really like him or did I just get caught up in my own flirt game?

- Just because he was flirt worthy, is he worthy to possess me? How am I going to feel about this ten minutes afterward?

Once you've decided to commit to the sexual experience, now you can really get into the hard-core part of flirting. Here's where the boundaries of "Is it flirt or foreplay?" really come into play.

⤳ He follows you into the bathroom or the bedroom or any room redolent with the heavy portent of intimacy. Prepare to be taken! Again, don't expect much in the way of conversation. When a man really wants you and is ready to have sex, talking is really the last thing on his mind.

How to Show Him You Want Him

You're sure he wants you . . . or at least you think you're sure. In reading any man, it's not always so easy to tell. Men are tricky. Sometimes they have had too much to drink or they are concerned about mechanical failures. Theirs, I mean! Still, your intuition tells you that you've passed beyond the point where you think you're going to be embarrassed if you make a strong physical move. What are those moves? How can you let him know unequivocally that you're red-hot and ready to go?

It's pretty easy to telegraph to a guy your arousal. If he's got any smarts at all and hasn't had five martinis to drink, he will know you're hot for him just because of the way you're looking at him or how close you're standing. An astute guy who knows a thing or two about unconscious body language can even read your pupils to gauge their dilation and know exactly how excited (or nervous) you are. Your nostrils may even be slightly flared, a definite indicator of physical arousal. Other signals can be that you can't keep your hands off him or that you want to be with him all the time. When everything about your behavior shows a man that you're throwing yourself at him, he can either take you up on your offer or he can store this information in the back of his own mental file cabinet for use at another time. Men who know a woman really wants them don't always act on that knowledge immediately. But they never forget that they know it.

Here are some urgent and not so urgent ways to tell a guy you physically desire him:

⟶ SAY, "YOU'RE MAKING ME HOT." This is different than saying, "You're hot," or "You're a hottie." Those comments are general. This comment is specific. You're telling him that he is making you feel warm, melting, ready to hop into bed with him. There's no ambiguity here. This is a red-letter invitation. Right up there in potency is, "I'd like to see you naked," or "I was wondering what you're like in bed." Say these phrases and you're bound to find out!

⟶ TOUCH HIM. You know where. Even lightly brushing your fingertips across the front of his pants in the area of the fly is a direct invitation to pleasures of the flesh. If he doesn't get hard immediately, don't panic. Your behavior might have simply surprised him. Give him a minute to get used to the idea that you're a bit of a sexual aggressor. Don't be surprised if before the evening's over, he utters his request to have you tie him up or spank him!

⟶ If you're out in public and you're feeling so randy that you can't wait to get home to get him between the sheets, lead him to the bathroom (this only works if it's a single—don't try this in a communal restroom!) and cloister yourselves behind closed doors. Start kissing him the moment you hear the lock turn and the rest will evolve as expected.

⟶ Write your desires down on a slip of paper and pass it to him. The written word is a powerful thing. You don't have to use raunchy language. Sometimes all you have to do is scrawl on a napkin, "My place, or yours?"

TAKING HIM HOME

When you're out in public with a guy and the two of you have decided that you want to get naked together, there's always that bit of awkwardness, those minutes that get bracketed between the heat of "Let's bail this party and run back to your place for sex," and "We're having sex." For whatever it's worth, if you have to take a forty-minute ride on public transportation or walk up more than six flights of stairs, expect for some of the heat to cool off. You'll have to work on it a bit to reignite the fire. In general, physically moving yourself from one place to another for the purpose of making love requires that you employ your most important flirting skills to keep the iron in the fire, lest time and distance let things cool off too much.

Here's some fun things to do to keep the embers of lust glowing:

⟶ Make out passionately in the car or the cab. If one of you is driving, save all your kisses for the red lights.

⟶ Keep up a constant stream of sexy talk while you're in transition from the place you've just been and the place you are going. Talk about how hot you are and how much you want him. This is definitely not the time to begin discussing the social foibles of all your comrades unless their foibles fall under the heading of Sexual Adventure. Remember that any talk about sex is sexy and an aural aphrodisiac!

⟶ Take off one fairly intimate garment, like your stockings, and leave them in plain view. Men get turned on by the promise of undress. They even find the word *undress* very sexy!

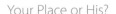

Your Place or His?

Where you go to be intimate really affects your flirtability quotient. Environment has a huge effect. At your own place you naturally feel more relaxed, more in control, more confident about what's going to happen. You know where the bed is, how warm the water in your bathtub or shower is, and you sort of know what's in the refrigerator for an après sex snack. You've also got your arsenal of aids and props like your equestrian helmet that hangs on the post of your bed that you can put on to flirtatiously pretend to "ride" him. His place is a different story. His bathroom may be so grungy that it makes you feel anything but flirtatious. It's not really flirty to start hauling out the heavy-duty industrial-strength cleaners to scrub down the shower stall or swab the toilet—at least not until after you've had sex, anyway. How should you act flirty in an unknown male environment? Try these tips:

····> Peel off most of your clothes and ask to borrow his shirt. Men love seeing a girl who is otherwise nearly naked wearing their stuff.

····> Offer to make the two of you a drink. Play cocktail waitress in your undies. That's always a hit!

····> While he's rummaging around in his CD collection, hop into his bed. Seeing you all cozy and waiting there for him is a total rush for a guy.

Flirty Foreplay

Once you're in the bedroom, the lines between flirtation and foreplay become a little blurred. But why shouldn't you have your flirt and your foreplay, too? Flirtation is a kind of tease and can be a means to an end—just like sexual foreplay. Real foreplay can be very flirtatious.

Great lovers like to incorporate elements of tease into presex. A big buildup not only makes lovemaking last longer, but it actually heightens the intensity of physical pleasure. Certain sensual tips and tricks can be used to whet sexual appetite and enhance performance and pleasure. Here are some tips and tricks to try that will get you in the groove:

⟶ Incorporate a bit of massage into your physical teasing. Light flirty strokes on the insides of your partner's thighs (this works equally well for men and women) arouse all the nerve endings and act as a warm-up for the entire genital area. Add some pleasing-smelling lotion or aromatherapy oil to the equation and you'll really get your partner hot.

⟶ Tease your partner with your mouth. Explore all his erogenous zones, one by one, with your lips and tongue. Start with his earlobes, then work your way down the sides of his neck. Focus on his nipples next (don't rush!) before moving on to his lower belly. By the time you hit the area right below his bellybutton he'll be moaning and groaning. For the time being, don't go any lower—you're just flirting!

⟶ Flirtatiously torture him with a feather that you use to lightly stroke and tease his entire body. Have him lie on his back to do this. It's even more fun if you order him to keep his eyes closed!

Hot Kissing Techniques

There's more to making out than just kissing. If all you do is lock lips, you're missing out on a lot! Learn to kiss flirtatiously—here's how:

⟶ DON'T JUST KISS. Lightly nibble and bite your lover's lips while you're kissing him. "Lightly" is the operative word.

→ BE THE SEXUAL AGGRESSOR. Slip your tongue into his mouth before he does it to you. Most guys think that women are too passive sexually—surprise him with your bold move. Kiss him in surprising places. Everyone kisses their lover on the lips. Have you tried kissing your guy behind his knee or on the inside of his elbow?

→ EXPLORE HIS ENTIRE FACE WITH KISSES. Kiss his eyes, his nose, his cheeks, his eyebrows—and then his mouth.

→ KISS HIM WHILE YOU'RE STRADDLING HIM. Sit on top of him or wrap your legs around his middle if you're sitting and kissing in a chair. Really lean into him so that it feels like you're kissing him with your whole body. He'll love it!

BEYOND MAKING OUT: FLIRTATIOUS FOREPLAY GUARANTEED TO DRIVE YOU BOTH WILD

Some of the best sex occurs long before penetration. Guys and girls can experience orgasm without penetration or actual sex. In fact, some of the best orgasms are achieved long before (or instead of) intercourse. Take your time to enjoy all the intimacies two people can share with each other. If you compare a long bout of passion to a six-course repast, you will see that there is nothing to be gained by rushing madly into the main part of the meal.

Petting

Petting is an incredibly sensual erotic experience. Petting involves touching and stroking every part of your partner's body—especially the most sensitive spots! If you don't know your partner very well, these tactile initial forays into his private areas should be done very slowly. When

HOW DO YOU KNOW YOU'VE BEEN FLIRTING UP
THE WRONG CYBERGUY?

How do you know if you've been flirting with a firecracker or a dud when you're online? Check out what some of these real women had to say:

1. You ask him where he lives and he says Minnesota, but he doesn't know where St. Paul is.

2. When he tells you he's married.

3. Cybersex comes before phone sex, doesn't everybody know that?

4. He types "BRB" (be right back) but all night long you never see hide nor hair of him.

5. You check his profile and discover he's really a she.

6. He says he has to go because his wife/mother/three-year-old daughter just came into the room.

7. He keeps calling you "Girlie" even though three times you told him your name.

8. He hasn't gotten the hang of how to use Instant Messaging.

9. You ask what he looks like and he tells you his body double is a "roughed-up Mr. Potato Head wearing boots." Or he writes, "I look just like Jude Law," when everyone knows the only person who looks like Jude Law is . . . Jude Law.

10. If he doesn't suggest phone sex immediately, he's definitely the wrong guy!

you don't know someone all that well, it's hard to know exactly where he likes to be touched or how. Take your cues on how you're doing by his response. If he gets tense when you touch one part of his body, move away from it and touch him someplace else.

Most men love it when a woman pets them in their pubic zone right away. Guys are really happy when a woman makes the first move to handle their penis. What they hate is to have to beg. Start out with a light touch and gradually increase the pressure. Some men enjoy quite a bit of squeezing and vigorous stroking, while others prefer a lighter touch. Ask your partner to show you how he pleasures himself and then imitate his hand motions. Copycat him and you can't go wrong!

Heavy petting usually means digital insertion or penile manipulation meant to bring the other person to climax. Tell your partner how you like to be touched and make sure you find out how he likes to be touched, too. Communication is essential, because every person is unique and different. Don't hesitate to give gentle directives, or show each other how you like to pleasure yourself. Demonstrate your private techniques in front of each other, or whisper special requests in the other person's ear. Those are two very personal and superhot ways to express your desires.

Frottage—which comes from the French word for "rubbing"—is best done when both people are nearly naked. (Really drive him crazy by doing all this rubbing while your underpants are still on.) No penetration or insertion here. Just two hot and close-to-naked people lying side by side or on top of each other, flesh pressing against flesh. Engaging in all the usual sexual movements—that is, humping, grinding, and basically everything you did with your boyfriend when you were both virgins—is what frottage is all about, and it's very, very hot!

Time-Honored Bedroom Tricks

Of course, you don't have to reinvent the wheel here. Using any of these time-honored tricks will heat things up quite nicely:

---> Ice cube anyone? Run an ice cube over your partner's super-heated body. This is a great thing to do on a hot, sweaty night when neither of you has air conditioning! Or put an ice cube in your mouth and then tease your partner with your mouth in an erogenous zone. This is mind blowing!

---> Whipped cream and chocolate sauce are really fun to lick off another person. You might want to do this in a motel room where you're not responsible for cleaning up the mess you make out of the sheets!

---> A light blindfold to cover your partner's eyes is very thrilling. When he can't see what you're about to do to him, it somehow heightens every experience. You don't need a real blindfold to do this. Any kind of scarf will do! Even if all you are doing is kissing or tonguing him on different parts of his body, his own anticipation just triples the excitement because he can't see what's coming next.

FLIRTING DURING SEX

You don't have to stop flirting just because you're finally "doing it." Even though we talked in the beginning of the book about flirting being "sex lite," real sex can include flirting and flirtatious behavior. In fact, that's what keeps it alive and interesting. Try these sexy tips for adding a dimension of flirtation to your lovemaking—you won't be disappointed!

Teasing Movements

The teasing doesn't have to stop because sex begins. Make every movement long and slow and drawn out. Make your partner beg for it—that's when he'll appreciate it most!

Keep on Kissing

That's right—why stop now? So many people think of kissing merely as foreplay. Don't! Continue kissing (and caressing) throughout the entire sex act. Your mouth on mouth connection will intensify every movement and keep things extra hot!

Start, Stop, Then Start All Over Again

Just because you've begun doesn't mean you have to race to the finish line. Tease and flirt with your partner by starting, stopping, and then having the fun of starting all over again. This is a natural thing to do when you're going to have sex for a good long time and enjoy lots of positions.

Flirty Dirty Talk

Men do love it when a woman talks trash in bed. Don't hold back a single thought running through your head. Tell him exactly what you like and what it feels like when he's doing what he's doing to you. If your talk turns a bit racy or even to hard-core smut, never mind—just say whatever filthy thing leaps into your head. Express yourself! Trust me, he'll love it.

READING HIS BODY LANGUAGE DURING SEX

Interpreting body language in bed is really pretty easy if you know what to look and listen for. You're making love to a guy. You're feeling pretty great, but how do you know that he's enjoying what you're doing? What messages is his body sending you?

You know he's having a great time if he does any or all of the following:

⟶ Moans and groans in ecstasy

⟶ Squeezes you tightly and won't let go

⟶ Leans back, closes his eyes, and emits sounds of intense pleasure as you're pleasuring him with your mouth

⟶ Grabs your buttocks and pulls you closer

⟶ Thrusts his hips spasmodically

⟶ Relinquishes all control of the situation and lets you take charge

⟶ Hugs you close to him afterward and tells you, "That was so good."

Celery isn't just low in calories. It looks hot in a woman's hand. Celery's very long, straight, basic phallic silhouette makes it the perfect flirt accessory/visual. But the green stalk has other erotic qualities as well. Since celery seeds are rich in vitamins A, C, B, and D and are loaded with minerals, this vegetable deserves its reputation for being a true food of love.

What about you? How do you let him know without speaking that he's giving you what you need or want?

A lot of women who are truly flirt experts suddenly turn shy when a man gets them into bed. Without their usual armor of hair, clothes, flirt buddies by their side, beards, a timetable, and a game plan—naked and alone with a man—they feel out of their element, vulnerable! Even when they know how to ask for what they need in bed from their partner, they suddenly turn shy about physically expressing themselves.

It's too bad when this happens because communication—verbal and nonverbal equally—is the key to sexual fulfillment and happiness. It's too simple to just tell yourself to relax, although relaxation is key. Your body language should be a form of communication with your partner to help him know that he's pleasing—and ideally, it should be spontaneous. In a perfect world you would just let go and let your natural instincts do the talking for you.

But since it's not a perfect world, what can you do to let your partner know that he's really ringing your bell?

---> Open your legs wide, really wide. It's the international signal that your mind and body are wide open and he should come on in.

---> Try not to tense up. It's inevitable that a new partner is going to touch you somewhere or somehow that you don't really like. And when that happens, you're going to freeze. Deliberately unthaw your body and gently direct that person to another prime spot. He'll have noticed your tension and hopefully will avoid that spot! Or, he'll coax you through it while he's touching or pleasuring you in that spot, relaxing you so that you can work through that pleasure barrier.

⤳ Lift your hips to meet his thrusts. Don't lie there like a log. It indicates disinterest!

Sex is like two people dancing. Don't step on each other's toes, try to follow the other person's rhythm (or establish the rhythm and be the leader yourself), and avoid jabbing the other person with your elbows. Sex can be clumsy. Work together to make it less so!

APRÈS SEX

What happens after sex is almost as important as sex itself. The two of you have just shared an incredibly intimate experience together. Hopefully it was hot, erotic, and maybe even romantic! How do you keep the good vibration going and an upbeat mood after the sex is over? The answer lies in the flirt.

Sexy, Flirty Things to Do Immediately After Sex

Cuddle a Little

Unless he's the type of guy who goes right to sleep after sex, engage in a little pillow talk. Keep it light and flirtatious. A simple "*Um,* that was wonderful" on your part will most certainly do.

If he is the type of guy who immediately falls asleep, don't fight city hall. Curl up and go to sleep for a few minutes alongside him. Don't be surprised if you do fall fast asleep. Orgasm is a natural aid to sound sleeping!

Do Something Together

After you've recovered, make a foray into the kitchen. Whip up a light repast to enjoy together. Keep the flirt vibe going by engaging in lots of touches and physical teasing.

If it was daytime or early evening sex, do something together afterward. It could be something as simple as taking a walk. Or maybe the two of you could make a run to the video store so you can spend a few more fantastic hours together. Rent a flirty movie that both of you want to see. *Chasing Amy* or *High Fidelity* are two good picks.

Dos and Don'ts for Après Sex

There are flirt enhancers and there are flirt killers in after-sex etiquette. Consult this list of Dos and Don'ts for what to do after you and he have made love so that you don't find yourself wondering what the heck went so wrong when up to that moment, everything seemed so right.

⋯⋯> DO thank the other person for the experience. Every lover, including a one-night stand, wants to be appreciated.

⋯⋯> DON'T start in with a litany of complaints about what he did or didn't do. This is just a total bummer.

⋯⋯> DON'T go into the bathroom and spend a half-hour in there cleaning up. If you want to take a shower, invite him in.

⋯⋯> DON'T get mad at him if he falls asleep right afterward when you're energized and ready to rock 'n' roll. Every person responds to orgasm differently. Give him fifteen minutes to take a nap before you start banging the pots and pans around or announcing you need a trip to the mall.

---> DO act friendly and upbeat to the man who just made love to you. Hopefully he worked hard to give you his best.

---> DON'T ask to use his toothbrush unless he offers it to you first.

---> DO continue to be your most adorable flirtatious self so that he can't wait to get you back in bed with him again!

CHAPTER 13

FLIRTATIOUS EXITS HE'LL NEVER FORGET

Get *your* tongue out of *my* mouth— I'm kissing you *goodbye.*

There comes a time in every flirt when it's just time to move on, walk away. This happens either because it's just time to go—maybe it was a quick flirt and now you've got to catch a plane—or this is a flirt of long duration but something has gone sour or awry. Whatever the reason, what you want to do is leave a memorable and lasting impression on your Flirt Object, a parting he won't soon forget.

So how do you take your leave (and remember to *always* leave before the guy does) in a way that makes him not be able to stop thinking about you—a last look or phrase that leaves him hungering for more?

Here are some real-life tips from Certified Flirtation Experts:

"I would just give someone I wanted to see again a really long, steamy kiss. Maybe follow it up with a sexy e-mail later."

—June

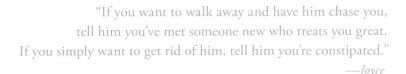

*"If you want to walk away and have him chase you,
tell him you've met someone new who treats you great.
If you simply want to get rid of him, tell him you're constipated."*

—*Joyce*

*"The first night I met my future husband he said to me, 'I'm in the
book.' My response to that was to let him know a day would never
be cold enough in hell for me to call a man who was 'in the book.'
He called me in no time."*

—*Helen*

THE EXIT STRATEGY

A wise flirt always knows when her meter is running out. When it's time to go, it's time to go! Maybe you ditched your date and you've got some repair work to do with him. Maybe you've got a plane to catch. Or maybe the flirt has gone as far as it can go for that moment but you're hoping for more. You hope you haven't seen or heard the last from this person who has totally enchanted you! Now how do you seal the deal and captivate him?

As any good flirt knows, the first thing you must have is an exit strategy. No, silly, this isn't taking notice of the actual building exits! Your exit strategy should be your arsenal of practiced lines to use alone or in conjunction with physical actions. These lines allow you to leave the scene of the flirt but still keep the mojo going. From verbal cues to body clues, this section will tell you everything you need to know to make an unforgettable exit.

You know it's time to end the flirt when:

- → You're losing him. He's stopped paying total attention to you and has begun to give another woman "the eye."
- → He seems more interested in what's on the tube than you in a tube top.
- → He's ceased noticing all the little things about you—like that you got your nose pierced or that you shaved your head.
- → He forgets your name and calls you by another one.
- → You've forgotten his name and call him by another one.

Your Verbal Au Revoir

Remember that it isn't *just* your shining eyes or winning smile or amazing figure that your Flirt Object remembers after you walk away. It's your last look or the last thing that you said that he will dwell on—even play again in his head over and over again hours if not days and weeks after you've left him. Imagine a man pondering your last phrase, your last lingering look for days after you've walked away from him. Pretty heady stuff, no? Here are some tried and true "I'm leaving now but I dare you to forget me" lines you can try for yourself:

- → It was really wonderful talking to you. I'd love to do it again sometime.
- → I really have to go now, but parting is (big grin) such sweet sorrow.
- → I love bumping into you like this. How can we bump more often?
- → Cya . . . I hope!
- → Oops, gotta run! My car is waiting. If I had known I would be having so much fun, I would never have ordered it!
- → It was so nice meeting you. You won't forget me, will you?
- → I am so sorry I have to leave now. I've had such a fantastic time talking with you. Next time I won't bring my boyfriend.

BOOTILICIOUS BODY LANGUAGE FOR SAYING GOODBYE

As witty and clever a conversationalist you may be, it's your physical persona that gets engraved in a guy's head after you've been flirting awhile with him. An hour later he won't remember the funny things you said (unless they're about something sexual—that, men remember), but he will have total recall of the way your body moved as you began walking away. Guys have a way of recalling even the smallest physical gestures—as long as they're directed their way!

The Half-Wave

This is as easy a place to start as any. It's a hand-job type of thing! Doing *it* is easy. Just raise your hand to around ear level, bend your elbow and keep it pressed close to your waist, and do the little ta-ta wavy thing using your arm only from fingertip to elbow. The half wave is really good. It's really, really flirty.

Air Kisses

Air kisses also make for a fine goodbye! Pretension aside, they do allow you to get right in there, right up to a person, but without any true physical contact. If you can, get right in near the ear, which happens to be a major erogenous zone. The double air kiss (the French Air Kiss) is even better. Here's how you do it so he'll never forget you:

1. Get close to him—about an eighth of an inch away from his cheek.
2. First, kiss his left cheek.
3. Next, kiss the right, then the left again.
4. Then kiss the right . . . well, you could keep going and going, but then you'd never stop, would you?

The Funny Goodbye

Funny is very sexy—and don't let anyone tell you differently! So how can you make a funny exit? If you can, end with a joke, then give him a playful jab to the ribs with your elbow before you sashay out of there. This gets you a little bit of physical contact—just enough to keep him interested until the next time.

The Farewell Handshake

Relax—this isn't as insanely boring as it sounds. If executed properly, it's actually one of the flirtiest goodbyes you can use. Leave him with a slight, lingering handshake. Slide your fingers through his, gently grasping his fingertips at the last second. This is a very *personal* touch. To be blunt, it's a lot like the first long caress a woman might give to a man's penis. Depending on how you use it, it's the kind of farewell handshake that could very well give him a hard-on. Talk about a sexy exit!

OTHER FLIRTY FAREWELL MOVES

There's certainly no limit to the flirty moves you can do—go where your imagination takes you! However, here are a few more just to send you on your way properly.

Coat Check

Ask a man to help you on with your jacket. This is a memorable and captivating move, and there's a lot of touching that can happen just by putting on a coat! Or you can try a variation and reach over yourself and touch something on *him*—adjust a scarf, maybe, or brush off a piece of lint.

IS HE OR ISN'T HE:
A CHECKLIST!

You've just spent the last half-hour flirting with a guy, and it's almost time to go now. So is your flirting working or are you back to square one? Guys give off so many signals that it's easy to get confused! Even though the two of you have been cozied up with your drinks at a cute table for two, even though he's tilting his head toward you, looking like he is listening to your every word, his eyes are staring at every pair of swiveling hips roaming the room. This simple checklist will help you determine where you're really at with a guy. That way, when you take your leave, you'll know if you should make a repeat performance or move on to the next flirtatious encounter.

He is into you if:

- He never takes his eyes off you, even when you're telling him about your mother.
- He talks to you with his hands, which, by the way, shouldn't be climbing under your skirt (in public, anyway).
- His face grows more animated the longer you are talking.
- He can't stop smiling at you.
- He brushes a stray piece of hair off your face just to have an excuse to touch your skin and make a little flesh on flesh contact.
- He calls you at random moments of the day just to say hi.

- He sends you text messages during your business meeting even though you told him you're not taking any calls.
- When you say you want to be left alone because you've got the flu, he comes over with chicken soup and a romantic comedy.
- He tells all his friends about you and acts a little jealous if they try to flirt with you.

On the other hand, he's not really into you if:

- His eyes roll back in his head whenever you start telling him about your family.
- He crosses his arms over his chest when you're together or taps his fingers on the table.
- He only smiles at you when you've spilled something on yourself.
- He never touches your hair, ever.
- He acts annoyed when you call him even if he still calls you to ask you out.
- He never sends you a text message or leaves cute messages on your voice mail.
- When you say you're sick and want to be left alone, he leaves you alone.
- He not only introduces you to his friends—he tries to set you up with them for future dates.

Face to Face

Another great exit move that works if you're very familiar with your Flirt Object is touching his face when you're saying goodbye. You can briefly brush your fingertips over his cheek in a soft caress or pretend to see a tiny crumb on the corner of his lip that you just have to remove.

Rear View: Perfecting Your Getaway Walk

Remember that when you actually walk away, your rear is the last thing that he's going to see. So be sure to use your booty (and more) to leave a lasting impression. *Hmm.* Bet you never thought of it that way, before, did you? The secret? Be prepared. While you can't always orchestrate the perfect exit, you can try to control what he's going to see. For example, when you're getting ready to go out, pay as much attention to your backside as you would to your front.

> ····⟩ Is your hair the way you want it, both front and back?
> ····⟩ Do your pants fit you right? Remember, guys love VPL (visible panty line), so don't worry if you've got it!
> ····⟩ Are your shoes snazzy, or are they too run down at the heel?
> ····⟩ Is your posture perfect?

Keep in mind how you're going to look walking away, and don't be afraid to work it a little bit. Swing your hips just a little—or, if you're tall and leggy and people think you're a model, swing 'em a lot! No matter how tall or small you are and no matter what you're wearing, if you can channel some Runway Model into your getaway walk, that's marvelous! Study that cable show, *Full Frontal Fashion,* for tips. Once you've figured out the hip motion, don't be afraid to add a little hair toss. If you want a guy to remember you, give him a strong visual!

Scent of a Woman

A last word of advice: Perfume lingers in the air after the wearer has left, so always wear a delicious fragrance when you're in any Flirtation Situation. That way, you'll leave the Object of Your Flirtation with the memory of your sweet scent. It's a subconscious thing, but it's the thing that really gets under a man's skin! What was that old ad campaign for the perfume Windsong? "You'll always stay in my mind." What could be better than that?

Instant Exits—How to Say Your IM Goodbyes

There are several ways to say goodbye online when you're chatting on IM with someone. Of course, there's the very common, *TTYL*, which means "talk to you later," and *BRB*, which technically means "be right back," even if you're not going to be back for hours. (Lots of people leave their IM catcher open with just such a message in case somebody they enjoy an online flirt with wants to be in touch at crazy hours.) A girl can never go wrong signing off with a series of xoxoxox's, which is shorthand for hugs and kisses. *Cya* is casual and not a bad way to go if you only just began talking with someone. *Mwah* is another way to say farewell. It's an online kiss, comparable to the real-life air kiss. Try saying it phonetically. *Mwah*. Get it? Don't be afraid to use it unstintingly. You can get away with "kissing" someone in the virtual world when you'd never dare kiss him in person!

QUICK GETAWAYS

There will be times when you've been chatting/flirting with someone and you realize that you're just not that into him. At all. Of course, the best way to get out of an undesirable flirt situation is to be as polite as possible and take your leave. In that case, thank the person for their lovely conversation (in other words, lie!) and make your getaway. Walk away slowly and with assurance, even if you want to bolt.

However, if you put yourself in lots of different flirtation situations, you're bound to run into total jerks from time to time. Maybe he's rude, or maybe he's just totally insulted you. Whatever it is, you know you'd rather have a bikini wax than spend one more second in conversation with him. And you know you're *not* in a Miss Manners kind of mood. So if you're feeling a little feisty, try one of these incredible exit lines offered by real-life Flirtation Experts:

⤑ Excuse me, but your breath is killing me. I have got to go!

⤑ Sorry, but I simply must get away from you! Ta-ta!

⤑ Yes, darling, that was the funniest thing I've ever heard. What did you say again?

⤑ Would you mind terribly if I threw up on your shoes rather than having to leave?

⤑ I would love to stay and chat but I simply cannot bring myself to do that. Adios, amigo!

WHEN GOOD FLIRTS GO BAD

Unfortunately there comes a time in many good flirts when things just go bad. Deep south, down the tube, total negativity. Some great flirts, even good ones, just run their course. Maybe it's a duration thing, maybe the riffs have gone stale, or maybe you just don't find each other very flirt-a-licious anymore. It could be because your Flirt Object has evolved into a total jerk! When the flirt between you goes stone cold, activate these tips for handling last encounters so that you're not the one walking away with a bad taste in your mouth:

Watermelon is the secret weapon of every sex goddess. Your most personal bodily fluids and secretions taste and smell more delicious if you make a habit of snacking on this fruit. Watermelon juice is loaded with antioxidants. It also perfumes the system, leaving your juices sweet and mild.

···⟩ Regard him as though he is a stranger. Look at him coldly, even dispassionately. Be as objective as possible. Decide if you like what you see.

···⟩ If you're still even talking, listen to his words carefully. Don't hear just what you want to hear. Really listen. If necessary, when you get home, transcribe the conversation so that you remember his words and can look at them again in the clear light of day and not under a haze of candlelight and alcohol.

···⟩ Avoid rising to the bait by responding to taunts or negative teasing. You might be a formidable insult artist in your own right, capable of wiping up the floor with this guy, but that's not the direction your final flirtation should go. Is that how you want to be remembered? For hurling the last insult?

⟿ Whatever happens, don't break down in tears. There's nothing remotely flirtatious about a woman with salt water running down her face. Besides, tears spoil mascara and crying causes your eyes to swell up. You wanna look your best when you move on to the next opportunity. And that's the beauty of flirting. There is always a next opportunity. Out of the ashes, a phoenix rises. That would be a great flirt—like you!

FROM THE MOUTHS OF GUYS

For guys, it's always a guessing game between what's hot and what's not. Here are some of the exit lines guys got that were hot, and the lines they've given or gotten that say "Stay away!"

"This one hurt. A woman I'd been seeing for awhile told me she wanted to spend more time with her cat!"—Mr. X

"The last thing I recall about her is the way she said goodbye. She kissed me tenderly on the mouth and hugged me close to her body. I had no idea that the next words from her mouth would be, 'If only you were a little older, or richer, or both.'"—C.

"She took a long time getting dressed. It seemed like forever watching her button her coat. For some reason I couldn't take my eyes off her fingers, which were so close to her breasts. She said, 'I hope we run into each other sometime.' Unfortunately, we didn't."—Jay

"She made a quick turn, head over the right shoulder, slowly whipping her hair behind her, smiled, and said, 'Let's hook up!' I damn near cried!"—Kevin

A GLOSSARY
OF FLIRT EXPRESSIONS

LOTS OF FLIRTATIOUS EXPRESSIONS are used in this book telling you how to act and behave. These phrases and expressions may not be part of your normal vernacular, so here's a little dictionary to help you understand what they mean.

Certified Flirtation Expert: Any woman who has used flirting to her best advantage in all situations, and who is willing to share her sage advice with up and coming flirts.

Come-Hither Stare: The stare that states, unequivocally, that you want him and will stop at nothing to get him.

The Equitation of Flirtation: Flirting with a man as though you were hopping in the saddle and riding a horse.

Flirtastic: You're flirtastic when you're a flirt expert and you're right in the groove, plying your trade!

Flirtationally Inclined: One who is adept at acting flirtatious in any range of situations, from the important to the mundane.

Flirtation Gaze: This is where you fix your eyes on that other person and basically penetrate them. Yes! In a way, it's a sex act! You lock eyes with that person, if only for a few moments. This immediately telegraphs interest, plus they have to notice you. It's also a mind control thing. If your flirtation gaze is strong enough, they won't be able to get away.

Flirtation Object: This person is your flirt target, the recipient of your flirt efforts, the person you've selected as your flirt beneficiary. Also known as your Flirt Object, or the Object of Your Flirtation.

Flirtee: In a Flirtation Situation, the flirtee is the person who is being flirted with.

Flirter: In a Flirtation Situation, the flirter is the person in control of the flirt.

Flirting Him Up: You know the expression, "chatting him up"? Well, this is almost the same thing. Except you're not just chatting. You're flirting.

Flirting Mantra: Your Flirting Mantra is your own personal flirt rule that you repeat to yourself whenever you feel your flirt energy petering out. Your main mantra should be, "Flirt more, flirt more."

Flirting with Purpose: This is a specialized type of flirt designed to extract pertinent information from the Flirt Object, such as marital status, occupation, etc.

Flirt Jerk Guy: This guy started out fun when you began flirting with him, but after a little while you realize he's totally ass-a-holic.

Flirtspeak: This is the special language of flirting, which includes double-entendres, flirty expressions, and any body language that conveys a flirtatious message.

Flirt Worthy: A term generally used when seeking out a new Flirt Object. Is he worthy of your excellent flirting abilities? If so, he's a Flirt Worthy candidate.

Flirty Bath: Taken alone or with a Flirt Object, the purpose of this bath is to relax, feel great, and get in the mood!

Kneesies: A variation on the popular game of footsies, Kneesies involves lighthearted knee play under a table or at a bar.

Mirroring: This is a typically a psychological term. Flirtologically speaking, however, mirroring is when you copy the movements of your Flirt Object to make him feel more comfortable and like you're on the same wavelength.

Mona Lisa Smile: This is a very subtle smile. Its meaning is slightly inscrutable. Are you smiling because you're amused? Or are you smiling because you know you've won?

Outflirted: Similar to being "outsmarted," this occurs when a flirt is upstaged by the flirtatious antics of another woman. You know you've been outflirted when the person you've been flirting with gets one over on you. Or the woman you're co-flirting with in competition for the same guy is the one who gets to go home with him. It means you lose!

Photo Op: The moment seized upon by an aggressive flirter in which she has her picture taken with her Flirt Object, leaving him with a lasting impression (and image of her).

Refusal Flirts: This is the flirt that just says "no." But no in a playful way. Like, maybe no means yes.

Scene of the Flirt: The physical space in which the flirt originated.

Sideways Glance: This is an indirect gaze, another flirtatious thing you can do with your eyes. It's executed fast—now you're looking, now you're not. You do it out of the corner of your eye. Don't get caught!

Urban Flirtation Legend: Stories of outrageous flirtations that are passed down from generation to generation to keep the spirit of flirting alive.

index